MICROSOFT OFFICE
in easy steps

Stephen Copestake

COMPUTER STEP

In easy steps is an imprint of Computer Step
5c Southfield Road, Southam
Warwickshire CV33 0JH England
☎ 01926 817999

Reprinted 1997
First published 1996
Copyright © 1996 by Computer Step

Notice of Liability

Every effort has been made to ensure that this book contains accurate
and current information. However, Computer Step and the author
shall not be liable for any loss or damage suffered by readers as a
result of any information contained herein.

Trademarks

Microsoft® and Windows® are registered trademarks of Microsoft
Corporation. All other trademarks are acknowledged as belonging to
their respective companies.

For all sales and volume discounts please contact Computer Step on
Tel: 01926 817999.

For translation rights and export orders write to the address above or
Fax: (+44) 1926 817005.

Printed and bound in the United Kingdom

ISBN 1-874029-37-7

Contents

A Common Approach

This chapter shows you how Office provides a common look, so you can get started quickly in any module. You'll learn how to create new documents and open/save existing ones. You'll learn how to use the Shortcut bar to save time and energy, and also how to get information you need from Office's on-line HELP system.

Covers

Introduction

The Standard edition of Microsoft Office consists of four modules:

- Word – word-processor

- Excel – spreadsheet

- PowerPoint – presentation/slide show creator

- Schedule+ – contact/time manager

Three at least of these programs are leaders in their respective fields. The point about Office, however, is that it integrates the four modules exceptionally well. With the exception of Schedule+, which necessarily adopts a relatively individualistic approach, the modules share a common look and feel.

The illustration below shows the PowerPoint Presentation opening screen. Flagged are components which are common to Word and Excel, too (though they're not necessarily shown in the illustrations on page 9).

 Toolbars figure largely in Office. For more information, see the 'Toolbars' topic later.

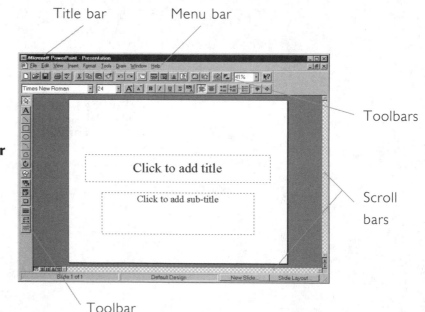

Title bar   Menu bar

Toolbars

Scroll bars

Toolbar

Compare this with the following:

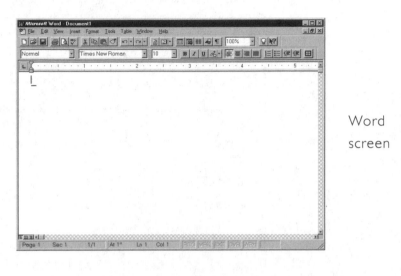

Word

screen

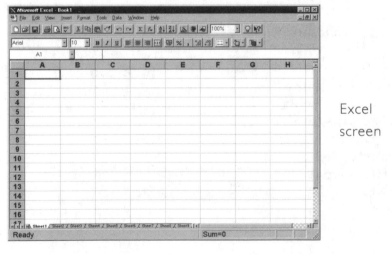

Excel

screen

There are, of course, differences between the module screens; we'll explore these in later sections.

Notice that many of the screen components are held in common. The purpose of this shared approach is to ensure that users of Office can move between modules with the minimum of readjustment.

Toolbars

Toolbars are important components in all four Office modules. A toolbar is an on-screen bar which contains shortcut buttons. These symbolise and allow easy access to often-used commands which would normally have to be invoked via one or more menus.

For example, Word's Standard toolbar lets you:

- create, open, save and print documents

- perform copy & paste and cut & paste operations

- undo editing actions

- customise the view level

- access Word's HELP system

by simply clicking on the relevant button.

Toolbars vary to some extent from module to module. We'll be looking at these in more detail as we encounter them. For the moment, some general advice.

Specifying which toolbars are displayed

In any Office module except Schedule+, pull down the View menu and click on Toolbars. Now do the following:

 Schedule+ has only one available toolbar. To display (or hide) this, pull down the View menu and click Toolbar. (No dialog appears.)

The Word, PowerPoint and Excel Toolbars dialogs vary slightly in terms of available options.

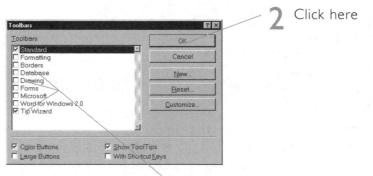

2 Click here

Click the toolbars you want to be visible

...contd

You can't add new buttons to the Schedule+ toolbar.

Adding buttons to toolbars

By default, the pre-defined toolbars which come with Office applications have only a small number of buttons associated with them (for instance, the Word Standard toolbar has 15). However, just about all editing operations you can perform from within Office menus can be incorporated as a button within the toolbar of your choice, for ease of access.

To do this, first make sure the toolbar you want to add one or more buttons to is visible (see page 10 for how to do this). Move the mouse pointer over the toolbar and right-click once. In the menu that appears, click Customize. Now do the following:

1 Ensure the Toolbars tab is active

Repeat steps 2 to 4 as often as necessary.

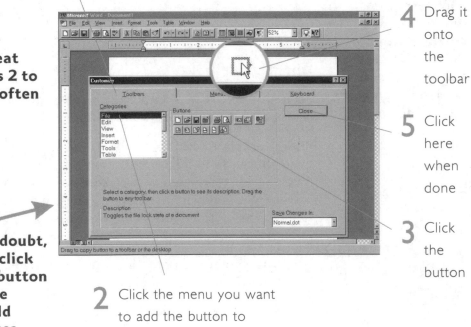

4 Drag it onto the toolbar

5 Click here when done

3 Click the button

2 Click the menu you want to add the button to

If in doubt, left-click any button in the dialog and hold down the mouse button; Office tells you what it does in the Description field.

Creating new documents

With the exception of Schedule+ (see Section 5), all Office modules let you:

- create new blank documents

- create new documents based on a 'template'

- create new documents with the help of a 'Wizard'

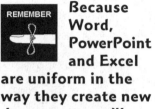

Because Word, PowerPoint and Excel are uniform in the way they create new documents, we'll look at this topic here rather than in the later sections, which are specific to each program. (However, see 'The AutoContent Wizard' in section 4 for specialised advice on creating new slide shows.)

Creating blank documents is the simplest route to new document creation; use this if you want to define the document components yourself from scratch. This is often not the most economical way to create new documents.

Templates – also known as boilerplates – are sample documents complete with the relevant formatting and/or text. By basing a new document on a template, you automatically have access to these.

Wizards are advanced templates which incorporate a question-and-answer system. You work through a series of dialogs, answering the appropriate questions and making the relevant choices.

Documents created with the use of templates or Wizards can easily be amended subsequently.

Both templates and Wizards are high-powered yet easy to use shortcuts to document creation. Office provides a large number of templates and Wizards. For example, Word offers Wizards which automate the production of newsletters, faxes, letters and memos, as well as numerous templates.

The topics that relate to the New dialog, templates and Wizards do not apply to Schedule+.

All three document creation methods involve launching the New dialog. This can be accessed:

- by using the Office Shortcut bar

- from within the modified Windows 95 Start menu

- from within the relevant Office program

Launching the New dialog

Use any of the following methods:

Using the Shortcut bar
Within the Office Shortcut bar, do the following:

If the Office toolbar isn't uppermost in the Shortcut bar, right-click on the bar. Click Office in the menu that appears. (For more help with the Shortcut bar, see later topics.)

Click here

Using the Start menu
When Office is installed, it amends the Windows 95 Start menu. Carry out the following procedure:

2 Click here

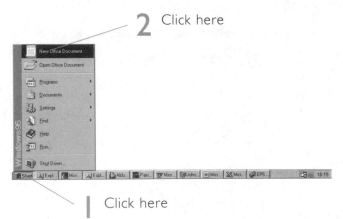

Click here

From within the program
In Word, Excel or PowerPoint, pull down the File menu and click New.

The following keyboard shortcut is available in Word, PowerPoint and Excel. Simply press Ctrl+N.

Excel's File menu

Using the New dialog

The form the New dialog takes depends, to some extent, on which method you use to launch it. If you invoke it by using the Shortcut bar or the Start menu, you get the full version which incorporates elements from Word, Excel and PowerPoint. You can then choose which type of new document you want to create.

If, on the other hand, you launch it from within the relevant program, you get a specific, abbreviated form.

Using the full New dialog

First launch the New dialog (see page 13 for how to do this). Then do the following:

To create a blank document, activate the General tab and click the Blank Document (Word), Blank Workbook (Excel) or Blank Presentation.pot (PowerPoint) icon.

The Preview section on the right provides an illustration of what your new document will look like (providing it's based on a template or Wizard).

Activate the relevant tab

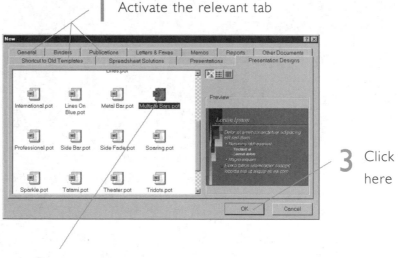

3 Click here

2 Click the blank document, template or Wizard you want to use

In the above illustration, a new PowerPoint presentation is being created, based on the supplied template MULTIPLE BARS.POT.

Using the program-specific New dialog

First launch the New dialog (see page 13). Then do the following:

Activate the relevant tab

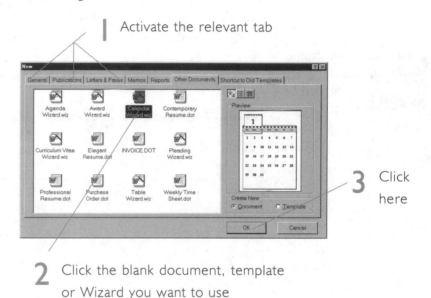

3 Click here

2 Click the blank document, template or Wizard you want to use

In the above illustration, a new Word document is being created, based on the Wizard CALENDAR WIZARD.WIZ.

Notice that the only new document options you can access in this form of the New dialog are Word-specific.

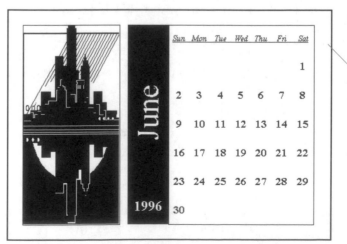

A calendar produced by Word's Calendar Wizard

Working with templates

If you elected to base your new document on a template, Office creates a detailed document complete with preset text and formatting.

The illustration below shows a new Excel worksheet based on the template BUSINESS PLANNER.XLT.

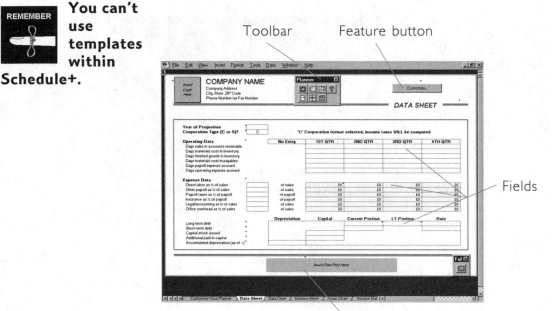

REMEMBER

You can't use templates within Schedule+.

Toolbar   Feature button

Fields

Feature button

This provides a good idea of how useful and sophisticated Office's templates are. In this case, Office has:

- created numerous pre-defined fields

- created several additional worksheets

- formatted the worksheet

- inserted special buttons which you can click to launch features directly

- launched a dedicated toolbar

Amend these as you see fit, then save the template as a document in its own right.

Working with Wizards

When you elect to create a new document with the help of a Wizard, Office launches a succession of dialogs. The illustration below is the first dialog when you run the Word Memo Wizard.

You can't use Wizards within Schedule+.

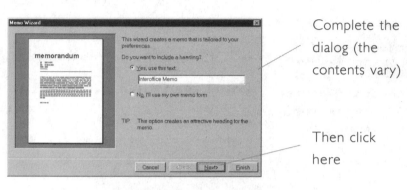

Complete the dialog (the contents vary)

Then click here

Office tells you when you've reached the final dialog by dimming the Next button.

Whichever Wizard you use, in whichever Office module (apart from Schedule+), complete the necessary fields and/ or click the necessary options. Then click Next to move on to the next dialog. Continue doing this until you reach the final dialog. Then do the following:

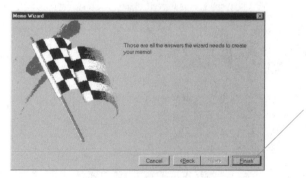

Click here

The end result of using a Wizard is the same as using a template: a feature-rich document which you can amend as necessary.

Opening Office documents (1)

We saw earlier that Office lets you create new documents in various ways. You can also open Word, Excel and PowerPoint documents you've already created:

- from within the Office Shortcut bar

For how to open an existing schedule in Schedule+, see the 'Logging on' topic in Section 5.

- from within the modified Windows 95 Start menu

- from within the relevant Office program

Using the Office Shortcut bar

Within the Office Shortcut bar, do the following:

Click here

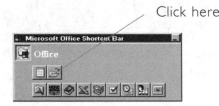

Using the Start menu

When Office is installed, it amends the Windows 95 Start menu. Carry out the following procedure:

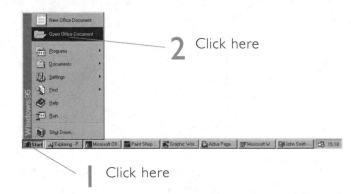

2 Click here

Click here

From within the program

In any module apart from Schedule+, pull down the File menu and click Open.

Opening Office documents (2)

Whichever method you use on page 18, Office produces the Open dialog. Carry out the following steps:

2 Click here. In the drop-down list, click the drive that hosts the document

HANDY TIP **If the relevant program isn't already running when you tell Office to open a file, it launches it automatically.**

5 Click here

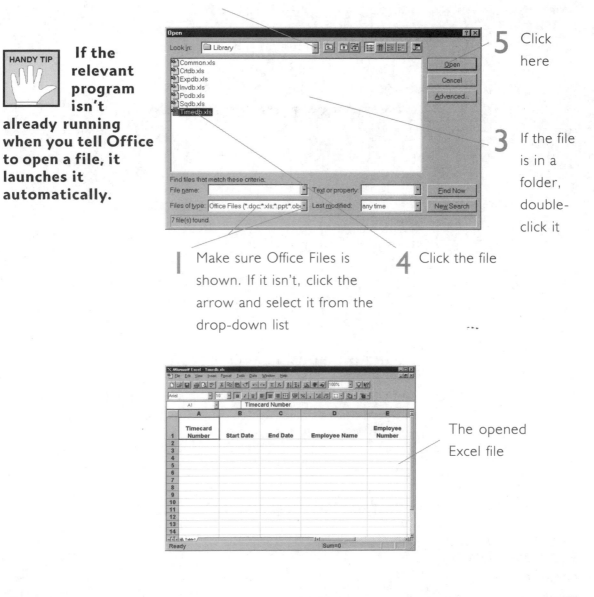

3 If the file is in a folder, double-click it

Make sure Office Files is shown. If it isn't, click the arrow and select it from the drop-down list

4 Click the file

The opened Excel file

Saving Office documents

It's important to save your work at frequent intervals, in order to avoid data loss in the event of a hardware fault or power interruption. With the exception of Schedule+, Office uses a consistent approach to saving.

Saving a document for the first time
In Word, Excel or PowerPoint, pull down the File menu and click Save. Or press Ctrl+S. Now do the following:

2 Click here. In the drop-down list, click the drive you want to host the document

5 Click here

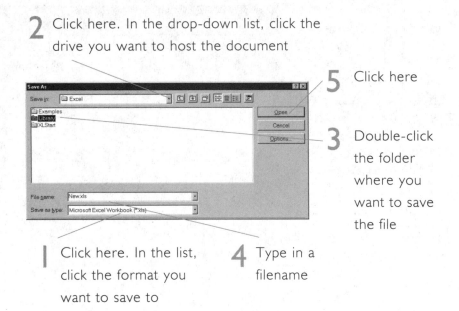

3 Double-click the folder where you want to save the file

1 Click here. In the list, click the format you want to save to

4 Type in a filename

Saving previously saved documents
In Word, Excel or PowerPoint, pull down the File menu and click Save. Or press Ctrl+S. No dialog launches; instead, Office saves the latest version of your document to disk, overwriting the previous version.

A shortcut you can use for either save method: in Word/ Excel/PowerPoint, click here.

This is PowerPoint's Standard toolbar

Using Office's HELP system

Office supports the standard Windows 95 HELP system. For instance:

Office calls these highly specific HELP bubbles 'ToolTips'. ToolTips are a specialised form of ScreenTips (see below).

*   moving the mouse pointer over toolbar buttons produces an explanatory HELP bubble:

*   moving the mouse pointer over fields in dialogs, commands or screen areas and right-clicking produces a specific help box. Carry out the following procedure to activate this.

Office calls these highly specific HELP topics 'ScreenTips'.

Left-click here for the specific help topic

Other standard Windows 95 HELP features are also present; see your Windows documentation for how to use these. Additionally, all the Office applications have in-built HELP in the normal way . . .

Office also has one unique HELP feature: the Answer Wizard.

The Answer Wizard

Normally, when you invoke a program's HELP system, you know more or less the question you want to ask, or the topic on which you need information. But what happens if neither of these is true?

Office offers one solution to this: the Answer Wizard. Its purpose is to allow you to enter questions in your own terminology. If you don't know the correct term for what you want to ask, you can put the question in your own words. The Answer Wizard then provides a list of available topics from which you can choose.

When you activate one of these topics, Office provides one of the following:

• an illustration

• a step-by-step guide

• detailed information

• a ScreenTip (see page 21)

Launching the Answer Wizard

There are various methods you can use:

• Pull down the Help menu in any Office application and click Answer Wizard.

• Alternatively, you can use the Standard toolbar in Word, PowerPoint or Excel (the illustration shows Word's) to launch the Answer Wizard. Simply do the following:

Double-click here

- Or do the following in the Office toolbar on the Shortcut bar:

Click here

Using the Answer Wizard

Office now launches the Help Topics dialog. Carry out the following procedures:

1 Ensure the Answer Wizard tab is active

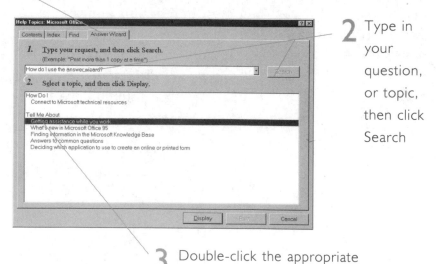

2 Type in your question, or topic, then click Search

3 Double-click the appropriate HELP entry

Office now launches the relevant HELP screen. When you've finished using this, press Esc or Alt+F4 to close it.

The Shortcut bar - an overview

As its name implies, the main function of the Windows 95 Taskbar is to switch between already open applications. Beyond this, it has some deficits. For instance, it doesn't let you start programs directly with a single click on a button (instead, you have to use the normal Start menu route, which requires several clicks and/or mouse movements). The Office Shortcut bar rectifies this omission. You can add buttons for any programs you want, and start them very quickly and easily.

The Shortcut bar also mimics the Taskbar. If a program is already open, clicking on its button on the Shortcut bar switches to it.

BEWARE

This only works with Office programs; if you try it with other programs, a second copy of the application launches.

We've already looked at how to use the Shortcut bar to create new documents or open existing ones. However, you can also determine the Shortcut bar's on-screen location. Additionally, you can have it display permanently, or 'auto-hide' it (where it only appears on screen when you move the mouse pointer to a specific screen area).

Toolbars

Buttons on the Shortcut bar are organised into specialist *toolbars*. The main toolbars are:

Office   has buttons relating to Office, and some system-specific buttons

Programs   by default, has buttons representing program folders

Desktop   has buttons representing folders on your desktop (e.g. My Computer, Inbox, My Briefcase)

Accessories   has buttons representing programs normally accessed from the Start/ Accessories menu (e.g. Notepad, WordPad, CardFile and Paint)

You can display as many, or as few, toolbars as you want.

Displaying Shortcut bar toolbars

Office uses a unique effect when you have more than one toolbar displayed at once on the Shortcut bar: it *layers* them.

Look at the illustration below:

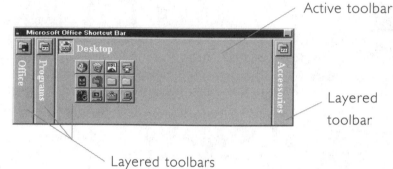

Active toolbar

Layered toolbar

Layered toolbars

Here, the Shortcut bar is 'floating'; for how to display it on the top, bottom, left or right of your screen, see the 'Specifying the Shortcut bar location' topic next.

To make another toolbar active, simply left-click on it.

Hiding/revealing toolbars

Move the mouse pointer over any toolbar and right-click once. Now do the following:

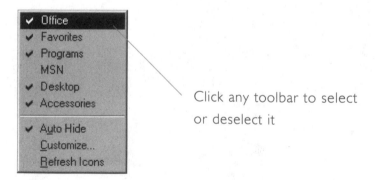

Click any toolbar to select or deselect it

Repeat this procedure for however many toolbars you want to hide or reveal.

Specifying the Shortcut bar location

You can have the Shortcut bar display on the left or right, or on the top or bottom of your screen. Alternatively, you can have it 'float' on screen, as a separate window.

Use whichever method is most convenient for the task in hand.

By default, the Shortcut bar docks on the right of the screen.

To move the Shortcut bar to the top, bottom, left or right of your screen (Office calls this 'docking'), move the mouse pointer anywhere over the Shortcut bar (but not over one of the buttons). Hold down the left mouse button and drag the bar to the appropriate screen area. When you release the mouse button, the bar 'docks' automatically.

This illustration shows the Shortcut bar when positioned at the top of the screen:

Double-click the title bar to have the Shortcut bar jump back to the last occupied position.

Shortcut buttons

Title bar

Layered toolbars

The Shortcut bar positioned horizontally, over PowerPoint

Auto-hiding the Shortcut bar

When it's floating, the Shortcut bar behaves much like any other window. For example, if it's minimised, clicking on the Shortcut bar button on the Taskbar maximises it. (For more information on how to interact with the Shortcut bar when it's floating, see your Windows documentation).

 You can only auto-hide the Shortcut bar if it's docked, not if it's floating.

If it's docked, on the other hand, the Shortcut bar can be made to conceal itself bashfully when not required. To do this, double-click in the Shortcut bar (but not on a button, or in the Title bar). Now do the following:

Ensure the View tab is active

Customize

View | Buttons | Toolbars | Settings

Color
Toolbar: Office
Color:
Change Color...
☑ Use Gradient Fill   ☐ Smooth
☐ Use Standard Toolbar Color

Options
☐ Large Buttons
☑ Show Tooltips
☐ Always on Top
☑ Auto Hide between uses
☐ Auto Fit into Title Bar area
☑ Animate Toolbars   ☐ Sound
☐ Show Title Screen at Startup

OK | Cancel

2 Ensure this is ticked

3 Click here

 **You can use a shortcut to auto-hide the Shortcut bar. Right-click over the bar; in the menu which appears, click Auto Hide. This procedure also revokes auto-hide, if required.**

Making the Shortcut bar reappear

To make the Shortcut bar visible again when you need it, simply move the mouse pointer to the edge of the screen where the Office Shortcut Bar is docked. For instance, if the bar was docked on the bottom of the screen, move the pointer as far down as it will go.

When you've finished, move the mouse pointer away from the docking area; the Shortcut bar disappears again.

Adding buttons to the Shortcut bar

You can add buttons that represent files to the Shortcut bar. These files can be program files, or just about any other kind of file.

Double-click in the Shortcut bar (but not on a button, or in the Title bar). Now do the following:

1 Ensure the Buttons tab is active

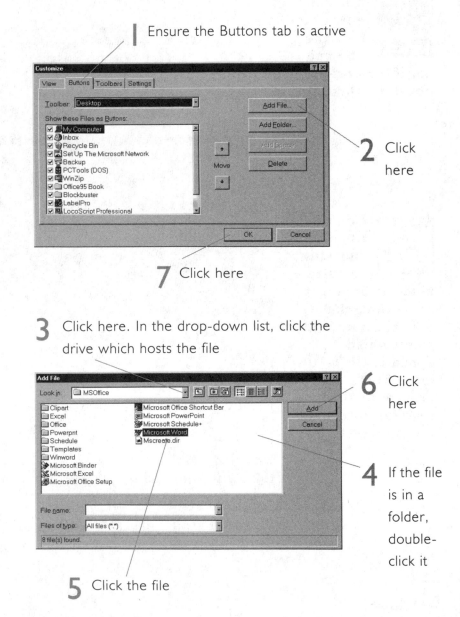

2 Click here

7 Click here

3 Click here. In the drop-down list, click the drive which hosts the file

6 Click here

4 If the file is in a folder, double-click it

5 Click the file

Word

This chapter gives you the fundamentals of using Word. You'll learn how to enter text and negotiate the Word screen. You'll also discover how to format text and apply text styles. Finally, you'll find out how to insert pictures and then customise page layout and printing.

Covers

The Word screen

Below is a detailed illustration of the Word screen.

Users of the CD version of Office can find this picture - TIGER.JPG - within the VALUPAK folder.

The Status bar displays information relating to the active document (e.g. what page you're on).

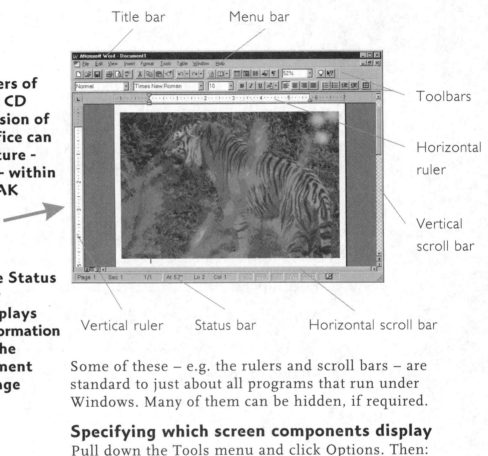

Title bar   Menu bar

Toolbars

Horizontal ruler

Vertical scroll bar

Vertical ruler   Status bar   Horizontal scroll bar

Some of these – e.g. the rulers and scroll bars – are standard to just about all programs that run under Windows. Many of them can be hidden, if required.

Specifying which screen components display

Pull down the Tools menu and click Options. Then:

Ensure the View tab is active

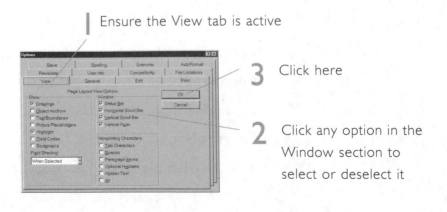

3 Click here

2 Click any option in the Window section to select or deselect it

Entering text

Word lets you enter text immediately after you've started it (you can do this because Word automatically creates a new blank document based on the default template). In Word, you enter text at the insertion point:

A magnified view of the Word text insertion point

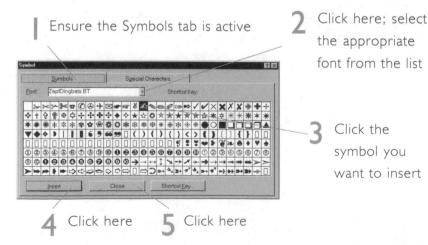

Begin entering text here

 Word has automatic word wrap. This means that you don't have to press Return to enter text on a new line; Word starts a new line for you automatically, when required. Only press Return if you need to begin a new paragraph.

HANDY TIP

Additional characters

Most of the text you need to enter can be typed in directly from the keyboard. However, it's sometimes necessary to enter special characters, e.g. bullets – for instance: ✍ – or special symbols like ©.

Pull down the Insert menu and click Symbol. Now do the following:

Ensure the Symbols tab is active

2 Click here; select the appropriate font from the list

3 Click the symbol you want to insert

4 Click here   5 Click here

Moving around in Word documents

You can use the following to move through Word documents:

- keystrokes

- the vertical/horizontal scroll bars

- the Go To dialog

HANDY TIP **To move to the location where you last made an amendment, press Shift+F5. You can do this as many as three times in succession.**

Using keystrokes

Word implements the standard Windows direction keys. Use the left, right, up and down cursor keys in the usual way. Additionally, Home, End, Page Up and Page Down work normally.

Using the scroll bars

Use your mouse to perform any of the following actions:

HANDY TIP **When you drag the box on the vertical scroll bar, Office displays a page indicator (magnified in the illustration) showing which page you're up to.**

Click anywhere here to jump to the left or right

Click anywhere here to jump to another location in the document

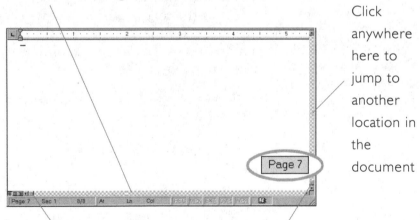

Page 7

Drag this to the left or right to extend the viewing area

Drag this up or down to move through the active document

...contd

Using the Go To dialog

You can use the Go To dialog to move to a variety of document locations. These include:

- pages (probably the most common)

- lines

- pictures

Pull down the Edit menu and click Go To. Now do the following:

| **You can use a keyboard shortcut to launch the Go To dialog: simply press Ctrl+G.**

1 Click the location type you want to go to

3 Click here

Go To

Go to What:
Page
Section
Line
Bookmark
Annotation
Footnote
Endnote

Enter Page Number:
15

Enter + and − to move relative to the current location. Example: +4 will move forward four items.

Go To
Previous
Close

2 Type in the specific location reference (e.g. a number if you selected Page in step 1)

There are some useful refinements:

- You can enter *relative* movements in step 2. For example, if you want to move seventeen pages back from the present location, type in -17. Or +5 to move five pages forward . . .

- To move to the next or previous instance of the specified location (i.e. without specifying a reference), omit step 2. In step 3, the Go To dialog is now slightly different; click Next or Previous, as appropriate. Click Close when you've finished.

Using views

Word lets you examine your work in various ways, according to the approach you need. It calls these 'views'.

Word has three principal views:

Normal

There is a fourth view which you'll use frequently: Print Preview. See later in this section for more information.

Normal View – the default – is used for basic text editing. In Normal View, most formatting elements are still visible; for instance, coloured, emboldened or italicised text displays faithfully. On the other hand, while pictures do display accurately, their precise location isn't reproduced: they simply appear on the left of the screen. Little attempt, too, is made to show document structure or layout; for example, headers and footers are invisible.

For these reasons, Normal View is quick and easy to use. It's suitable for bulk text entry and editing. Not recommended for use with graphics.

Page Layout

Page Layout view works like Normal view, with one exception: the positioning of items on the page is reproduced accurately. Headers and footers are visible, and can be edited directly; margins display faithfully; and pictures occupy their correct position on-screen.

In Page Layout view, the screen is updated more slowly. As a result, use it when your document is nearing completion.

Full Screen

When Full Screen view is active, you lose access to toolbars and scroll bars. However, you can still access the menus by using the keyboard (e.g. Alt+F to launch the File menu). Alternatively, move the mouse pointer to the appropriate location at the top of the screen and click.

Full Screen view isn't an alternative to Normal or Page Layout views; it's more of a supplement. Unless you have a particularly large monitor, you'll probably find that there are times when your screen is too cluttered. Full Screen view hides all screen components in one operation, thereby making more space available for editing.

Use Full Screen view when you need it, as an adjunct to Normal or Page Layout view.

Normal view

Page Layout view

Full Screen (with
Page Layout) view

Switching between Normal & Page Layout views

Pull down the View menu. Click Normal or Page Layout, as
appropriate (the view that is currently active has a bullet
against it).

Switching to Full Screen view

In either Normal or Page Layout view, pull down the View
menu and click Full Screen.

To leave Full Screen view, press Esc.

Changing zoom levels

The ability to vary the level of magnification for the active document is often useful. Sometimes, it's helpful to 'zoom out' (i.e. decrease the magnification) so that you can take an overview; at other times, you'll need to 'zoom in' (increase the magnification) to work in greater detail. Word lets you do either of these very easily.

You can do any of the following:

- choose from preset zoom levels (e.g. 100%, 75%)

- specify your own zoom percentage

- choose Many Pages, to view a specific number of pages at once

Setting the zoom level

Pull down the View menu and click Zoom. Now carry out steps 1 & 2 or 3 & 4 (as appropriate) below. Then follow step 5.

The Preview section on the right provides an indication of what the selected view level looks like.

Entries here must lie in the range 10%-200%.

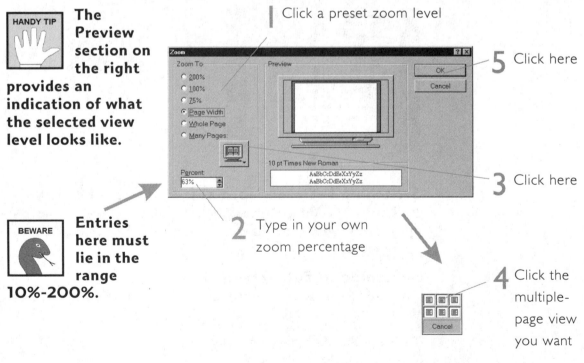

Click a preset zoom level

5 Click here

3 Click here

2 Type in your own zoom percentage

4 Click the multiple-page view you want

Formatting text - an overview

Word lets you format text in a variety of ways. Broadly, however, text formatting can be divided into two overall categories:

Character formatting

Character formatting is concerned with altering the *appearance* of selected text. Examples include:

- changing the font and typesize

- colouring text

- changing the font style (bold, italic etc.)

- underlining text

- applying font effects (superscript, subscript, small caps etc.)

Character formatting is a misnomer in one sense: it can also be applied to specific paragraphs of text.

Paragraph formatting

Paragraph formatting has to do with the structuring and layout of paragraphs of text. Examples include:

- specifying paragraph indents

- specifying paragraph alignment (e.g. left or right justification)

- specifying paragraph and line spacing

- imposing borders and/or fills on paragraphs

The term "paragraph formatting" is also something of a misnomer in that some of these – for instance, line-spacing – can also be applied to the whole of the active document rather than selected paragraphs.

Changing the font or typesize

Character formatting can be changed in two ways:

- from within the Font dialog

- (to a lesser extent) by using the Formatting toolbar

HANDY TIP

Word uses standard Windows procedures for text selection.

Applying a new font or typesize (1)

First, select the text whose typeface and/or typesize you want to amend. Pull down the Format menu and click Font. Now do the following:

Ensure the Font tab is active

HANDY TIP

Re step 3 – as well as whole point sizes, you can also enter half-point increments, i.e. Word will accept 10, 10.5 or 11, but not 10.75.

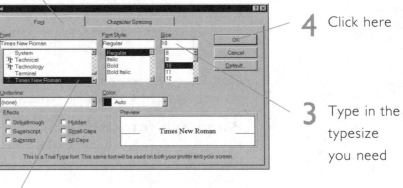

4 Click here

3 Type in the typesize you need

2 Click the font you want to use

HANDY TIP

If the Formatting toolbar isn't currently visible, pull down the View menu and click Toolbars. In the Toolbars field in the Toolbars dialog, click Formatting. Then click OK.

Applying a new font or typesize (2)

Make sure the Formatting toolbar is visible. Now select the text you want to amend and do the following:

Click here; select the font you want to use in the drop-down list

Type in the typesize you need and press Enter

Changing text colour

You can only change the colour of text by using the font dialog.

First, select the text you want to alter. Pull down the Format dialog and click Font. Now do the following:

Ensure the Font tab is active

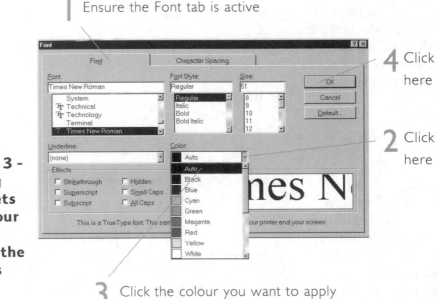

4 Click here

2 Click here

Re step 3 - clicking Auto sets the colour to black (unless you've amended the default Windows text colour).

HANDY TIP

3 Click the colour you want to apply

Verifying current text formatting

If you're in any doubt about what character/paragraph formatting attributes are associated with text, press Shift+F1. Now click in the text. This is the result:

How to verify text

Press Esc to return to normal text editing.

Changing the font style

The default font style is Regular. The additional font styles you can use depend on the typeface. For example, Times New Roman has Bold, Italic and Bold Italic. Arial Rounded MT Bold, on the other hand, merely has Bold and Bold Italic.

You can use the Font dialog or the Formatting toolbar to change font styles.

You can also use keyboard shortcuts: Ctrl+B to embolden selected text, Ctrl+I to italicise it.

Amending the font style (1)

First, select the text whose style you want to change. Then pull down the Format menu and click Font. Do the following:

Ensure the Font tab is active

The Preview section provides an indication of what the amendments you make look like.

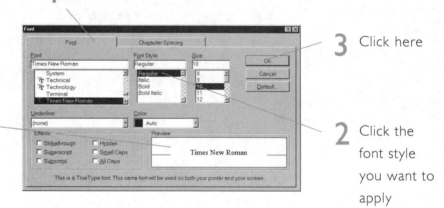

3 Click here

2 Click the font style you want to apply

If the Formatting toolbar isn't visible, pull down the View menu and click Toolbars. In the Toolbars field in the Toolbars dialog, click Formatting. Then click OK.

Amending the font style (2)

First, select the relevant text. Ensure the Formatting toolbar is visible. Then do the following:

Click here to embolden the text

| Normal | Times New Roman | 10 | B I U | |

Click here to italicise it

Underlining text

Word supports four kinds of underlining:

- Single

- Words Only

- Double

- Dotted

HANDY TIP

You can also use the following keyboard shortcuts: Ctrl+U for Single; Ctrl+Shift+W for Words Only; Ctrl+Shift+D for Double.

You can use either the Font dialog or the Formatting toolbar (it only supports Single) to underline text.

Underlining text (1)

First select the text you want to underline. Pull down the Format menu and click Font. Now do the following:

Ensure the Font tab is active

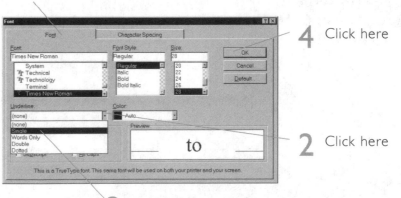

4 Click here

2 Click here

3 Click the underlining type you want to use

Underlining text (2)

First, select the relevant text. Ensure the Formatting toolbar is visible. Then do the following:

Click here

Font effects

The following are the principal font effects:

- *Strikethrough* – e.g. ~~font effect~~

- *Superscript* – e.g. f$^{\text{ont effect}}$

- *Subscript* – e.g. f$_{\text{ont effect}}$

- *All Caps* – e.g. FONT EFFECT

- *Small Caps* – e.g. FONT EFFECT

You can also use the following keyboard shortcuts: Ctrl++ for Superscript; Ctrl+= for Subscript; Ctrl+Shift+K for Small Caps; Ctrl+Shift+A for All Caps; Ctrl+Shift+H for Hidden.

In addition, you can mark text as hidden, which means that it doesn't display on screen or print.

You can only apply font effects from within the Font dialog.

Applying font effects

First, select the relevant text. Pull down the Format dialog and click Font. Then carry out the following steps:

Ensure the Font tab is active

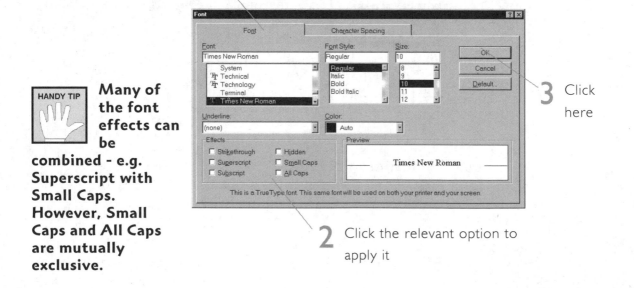

Many of the font effects can be combined - e.g. Superscript with Small Caps. However, Small Caps and All Caps are mutually exclusive.

3 Click here

2 Click the relevant option to apply it

Indenting paragraphs - an overview

You can achieve a similar effect by using tabs. However, indents are easier to apply (and amend subsequently).

Indents are a crucial component of document layout. For instance, in most document types indenting the first line of paragraphs (i.e. moving it inwards away from the left page margin) makes the text much more legible.

Other document types – e.g. bibliographies – can use the following:

- negative indents (where the direction of indent is towards and beyond the left margin)

- hanging indents (where the first line is unaltered, while subsequent lines are indented)

- full indents (where the entire paragraph is indented away from the left and/or the right margins)

Don't confuse indents with page margins. Margins are the gap between the edge of the page and the text area; indents define the distance between the margins and text.

Some of the potential indent combinations are shown in the illustration below:

> This paragraph has a full left and right indent. It's best, however, not to overdo the extent of the indent: 0.35 inches is often more than adequate.
>
>   This paragraph has a first-line indent. This type of indent is suitable for most document types. It's best, however, not to overdo the extent of the indent: 0.35 inches is often more than adequate.
>
> This paragraph has a negative left indent. It's best, however, not to overdo the extent of the indent: 0.35 inches is often more than adequate.
>
> This paragraph has a hanging indent. It's best, however, not to overdo the extent of the indent: 0.35 inches is often more than adequate.

left and right indent

first-line indent

negative left indent

hanging indent

Left margin (inserted for illustration purposes)

Right margin (inserted for illustration purposes)

Applying indents to paragraphs

Paragraphs can be indented from within the Paragraph dialog, or (to a lesser extent) by using the Formatting toolbar.

Indenting text (1)

First, select the paragraph you want to indent. Pull down the Format menu and click Paragraph. Now follow step 1 below. If you want a left indent, carry out step 2. For a right indent, follow step 3. To achieve a first-line or hanging indent, follow steps 4 and 5. Finally, irrespective of the indent type, carry out step 6.

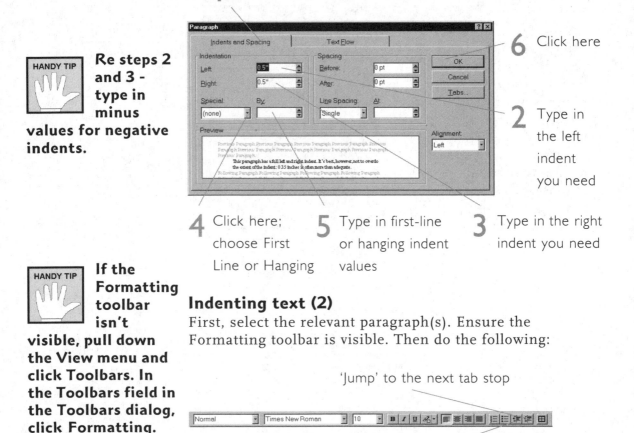

Ensure the Indents and Spacing tab is active

6 Click here

2 Type in the left indent you need

4 Click here; choose First Line or Hanging

5 Type in first-line or hanging indent values

3 Type in the right indent you need

Indenting text (2)

First, select the relevant paragraph(s). Ensure the Formatting toolbar is visible. Then do the following:

'Jump' to the next tab stop

'Jump' to the previous tab stop

Aligning paragraphs

Word supports the following types of alignment:

Left alignment
Text is flush with the left page margin.

Right alignment
Text is flush with the right page margin.

Justification
Text is flush with the left *and* right page margins.

Centred
Text is aligned equidistantly between the left and right page margins.

You can align text from within the Paragraph dialog, or with the use of the Formatting toolbar.

 You can only left- or right-align text if the Left and Right Indent values are set to Nil.

Aligning text (1)
First, select the paragraph you want to indent. Pull down the Format menu and click Paragraph. Now:

Ensure the Indents and Spacing tab is active

4 Click here

2 Click here

3 Click the alignment you need

 If the Formatting toolbar isn't currently visible, pull down the View menu and click Toolbars. In the Toolbars field within the Toolbars dialog, click Formatting. Click OK.

Aligning text (2)
Select the relevant paragraph(s). Then click any of these:

Left align   Right align

Centre   Justify

Specifying paragraph spacing

As a general rule, set low paragraph spacing settings: a little goes a long way.

Picas are an alternative measure in typography: one pica is almost equivalent to one-sixth inch. Picas are often used to define line length.

Word lets you customise the vertical space before and/or after specific text paragraphs. This is a useful device for increasing text legibility.

You can only set paragraph spacing from within the Paragraph dialog.

By default, Word defines paragraph spacing – like typesizes – in point sizes. However, if you want you can enter measurements in different units. To do this, apply any of the following suffixes to values you enter:

- in – for inches e.g. '2 in'

- cm – for centimetres e.g. '5 cm'

- pi – for picas e.g. '14 pi'

Applying paragraph spacing

First, select the paragraph you want to indent. Pull down the Format menu and click Paragraph. Now carry out the steps below:

Ensure the Indents and Spacing tab is active

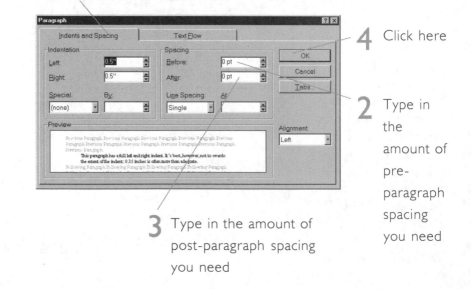

4 Click here

2 Type in the amount of pre-paragraph spacing you need

3 Type in the amount of post-paragraph spacing you need

Line spacing - an overview

It's often necessary to amend line spacing. This is the vertical distance between individual lines of text, or more accurately between the baseline (the imaginary line on which text appears to sit) of one line and the baseline of the previous.

Line spacing is also known as leading (pronounced 'ledding').

Word lets you apply a variety of line spacing settings:

Single
Word separates each line of type by an amount which is slightly more than the typesize. For example, if the text is in 12 points, the gap between lines is just over 12 points. Newspapers, particularly, use single line spacing.

This is Word's default.

1.5 Lines
150% of single line spacing.

Double
200% of single line spacing. Manuscripts of all descriptions are nearly always prepared with double line spacing.

At Least
Sets the minimum line height at the value you specify; Word can adjust the line spacing to fit the constituent character sizes.

Exactly
Sets the value you specify as an unvarying line height: Word cannot adjust it.

Multiple
Sets line height as a multiple of single-spaced text. For example, specifying '3.5' here initiates a line height of 3.5 lines.

Adjusting line spacing

First, select the relevant paragraph(s). Then pull down the Format menu and do the following:

HANDY TIP

If you've just created a new document, you can set the line spacing before you begin to enter text. Simply leave the insertion point at the start of the document, and then follow the procedures outlined here.

Click here

Now perform step 1 below. If you want to apply a preset spacing, follow step 2. To implement your own spacing, carry out steps 3 and 4 instead. Then follow step 5.

| Ensure the Indents and Spacing tab is active

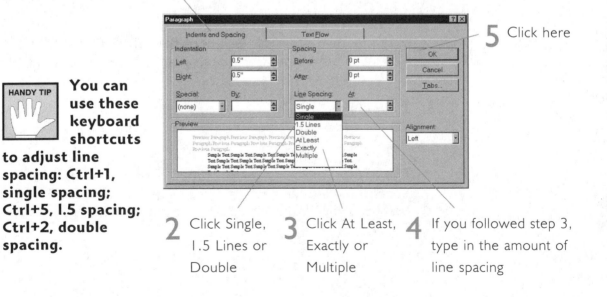

HANDY TIP

You can use these keyboard shortcuts to adjust line spacing: Ctrl+1, single spacing; Ctrl+5, 1.5 spacing; Ctrl+2, double spacing.

5 Click here

2 Click Single, 1.5 Lines or Double

3 Click At Least, Exactly or Multiple

4 If you followed step 3, type in the amount of line spacing

Paragraph borders

By default, Word does not border paragraph text. However, you can apply a wide selection of borders if you want. You can specify:

- the type and thickness of the border

- how many sides the border should have

- the border colour

- whether the bordered text should have a drop shadow

- the distance of the border from the text

Applying a border

First, select the paragraph(s) you want to border. Then pull down the Format menu and click Borders and Shading. Now do the following:

HANDY TIP **Re step 4 - click Shadow instead of Box if you want the border to have a drop shadow. Then proceed as normal.**

HANDY TIP **Use step 5 to deselect the top, bottom, left or right paragraph borders. If you want to deselect more than one, repeat step 5 as often as necessary.**

1 Ensure the Borders tab is active

7 Click here

4 Click here to border all four sides of the text

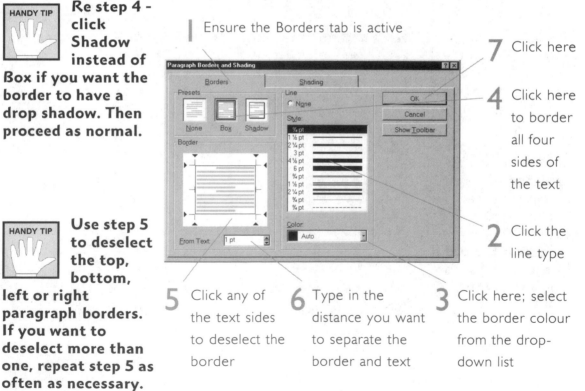

2 Click the line type

5 Click any of the text sides to deselect the border

6 Type in the distance you want to separate the border and text

3 Click here; select the border colour from the drop-down list

Paragraph fills

By default, Word does not apply a fill to text paragraphs. However, you can do the following if you want:

- specify the percentage fill (e.g. 20%)

- apply a simple pattern, if required

- specify the foreground fill colour

- specify the background fill colour

Applying a fill

First, select the paragraph(s) you want to fill. Then pull down the Format menu and click Borders and Shading. Now carry out step 1 below. Follow steps 2, 3 or 4 as appropriate. Finally, carry out step 5:

1 Ensure the Shading tab is active

5 Click here

HANDY TIP

Re steps 3 and 4, you can achieve unique blends by applying different foreground and background fill colours. Try reversing the order of these steps, too: this varies the result.

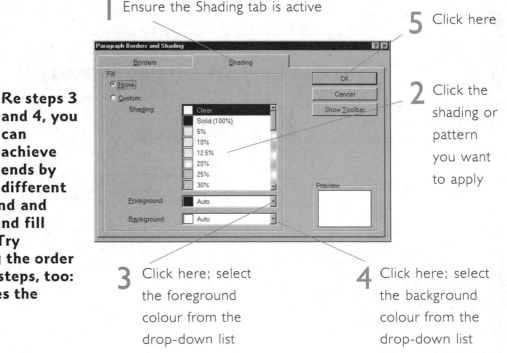

2 Click the shading or pattern you want to apply

3 Click here; select the foreground colour from the drop-down list

4 Click here; select the background colour from the drop-down list

Working with tabs

Tabs are a means of indenting the first line of text paragraphs (you can also use indents for this purpose).

Never use the Space Bar to indent paragraphs: spaces vary in size according to the typeface and typesize applying to specific paragraphs.

When you press the Tab key while the text-insertion point is at the start of a paragraph, the text in the first line jumps to the next tab stop. This is a useful way to increase the legibility of your text. Word lets you set tab stops with great precision.

By default, Word inserts tab stops automatically every half an inch. If you want, you can enter new or revised tab stop positions individually.

Setting tab stops

First, select the paragraph(s) in which you need to set tab stops. Pull down the Format menu and click Tabs. Now carry out step 1 below. If you want to implement a new default tab stop position, follow step 2. If you need to set up individual tab stops, carry out steps 3 and 4 as often as necessary. Finally, follow step 5 to confirm your changes.

When you've performed steps 3 & 4, the individual tab stop position appears here:

2 Type in the new tab stop default (e.g. 0.35")

5 Click here

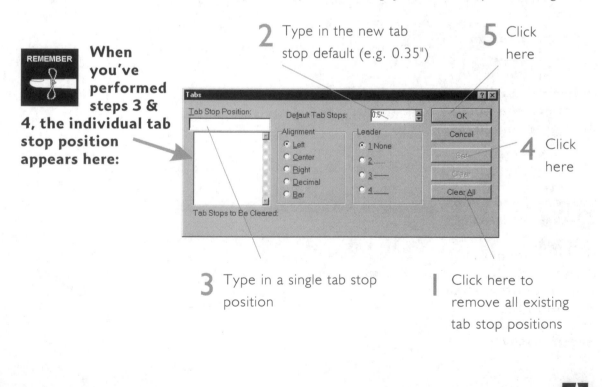

4 Click here

3 Type in a single tab stop position

1 Click here to remove all existing tab stop positions

Searching for text

Word lets you search for specific text within the active document. Even better, however, you can also search for character or paragraph formatting, either separately from the text search or at the same time.

For example, you can if you want have Word locate all instances of the word 'information'. Or you could have it find all italicised words, whatever they are. Similarly, you could have it flag all instances of '*information*'.

You can also:

- limit the search to words which match the case of the text you specify (e.g. if you search for 'Man', Word will not flag 'man' or 'MAN')

- limit the search to whole words (e.g. if you search for 'nation', Word will not flag 'international')

- have Word search for word forms (e.g. if you look for 'began', Word will also stop at 'begin', 'begun' and 'beginning')

- have Word search for homophones (e.g. if you look for 'there', Word will flag 'their')

 You can use a keyboard shortcut to launch the Find dialog: simply press Ctrl+F.

Initiating a text search

Pull down the Edit menu and click Find. Now do the following:

Type in the text you want to find

 When you follow step 3, Word launches a menu; click the relevant entry. Then complete the dialog which appears in the normal way.

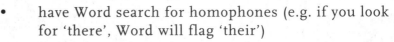

4 Click here to start the search

2 Specify the search parameters you need

3 Click here to search for formatting

Replacing text

When you've located text and/or formatting, you can have Word replace it automatically with the text and/or formatting of your choice.

You can customise find-and-replace operations with the same parameters as a simple Find operation. For example, you can have Word find every occurrence of '**information**' and replace it with '*information*', or even '*data*' . . .

Initiating a find-and-replace operation

First pull down the Edit menu and click Replace. Now follow steps 1 and 2 below. Carry out steps 3 and/or 4, as appropriate. Finally, follow either step 5 or 6:

You can use a keyboard shortcut here: simply press Ctrl+H.

REMEMBER

When you follow step 3, Word launches a menu; click the relevant entry. Then complete the dialog which appears in the normal way.

1 Type in the text you want to find

2 Type in the replacement text

5 Click here to replace the 1st instance of the specified text

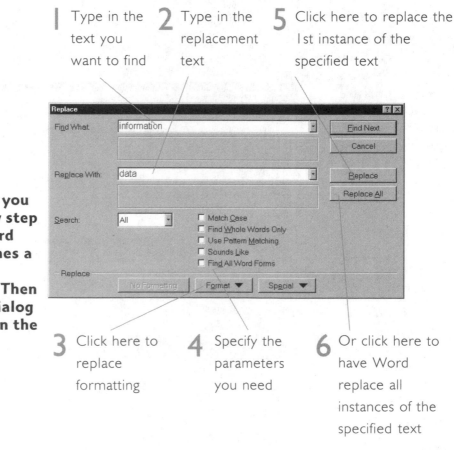

3 Click here to replace formatting

4 Specify the parameters you need

6 Or click here to have Word replace all instances of the specified text

Working with headers

You can have Word print text at the top of each page within a document; these are called 'headers'. In the same way, you can have Word print text at the base of each page; these are called 'footers'. Headers and footers are printed within the top and bottom page margins, respectively.

To edit an existing header, simply follow the procedures outlined here; in step 1, amend the current header text as necessary.

When you create a header, Word automatically switches the active document to Page Layout view and displays the Header and Footer toolbar.

Inserting a header

Move to the start of your document. Pull down the View menu and click Header and Footer.

Header text can be formatted in the normal way. For instance, you can apply a new font and/or typesize . . .

You can have Word insert a special code which automatically inserts the page number in the header - see step 3.

1 Type in the Header text

4 Click here to return to normal document editing

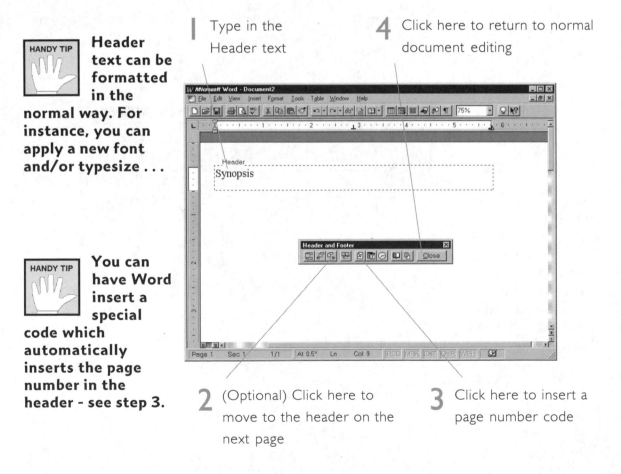

2 (Optional) Click here to move to the header on the next page

3 Click here to insert a page number code

Working with footers

When you create a footer, Word automatically switches the active document to Page Layout view and displays the Header and Footer toolbar.

To edit an existing footer, simply follow the procedures outlined here; in step 1, amend the current footer text as necessary.

Inserting a footer

Move to the start of your document. Pull down the View menu and click Header and Footer. Word launches the Header and Footer toolbar over the header area. To create a footer, do the following:

Click here

Footer text can be formatted in the normal way. For instance, you can apply a new font and/or typesize . . .

Word moves to the footer area. Now do the following:

2 (Optional) Click here to move to the footer on the next page

3 Click here to insert a page number code

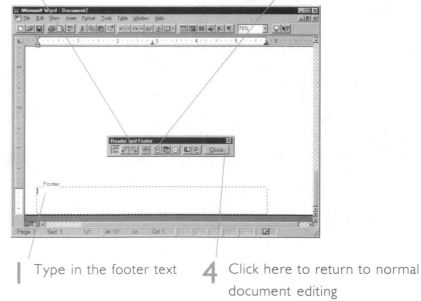

You can have Word insert a special code which automatically inserts the page number in the footer - see step 3.

| Type in the footer text

4 Click here to return to normal document editing

Undo and redo

Word lets you reverse – 'undo' – just about any editing operation. If, subsequently, you decide that you do want to proceed with an operation that you've reversed, you can 'redo' it.

You can even undo or redo a series of operations in one go.

You can undo and redo actions in the following ways (in descending order of complexity):

- via the keyboard

- from within the Edit menu

- from within the Standard toolbar

Using the keyboard
Simply press Ctrl+Z to undo an action, or Ctrl+Y to reinstate it.

Using the Edit menu
Pull down the Edit menu and click Undo ... or Redo ... as appropriate (the ellipses denote the precise nature of the action to be reversed or reinstated).

Using the Standard toolbar
Carry out the following actions:

If you select an early operation in the Undo or Redo lists, all later operations are also reversed or reinstated.

Click here to redo an action; in the drop-down list, select the relevant action(s)

Click here to undo an action; in the drop-down list, select the relevant action(s)

Text styles - an overview

Styles are named collections of associated formatting commands.

The advantage of using styles is that you can apply more than one formatting enhancement to selected text in one go. Once a style is in place, you can change one or more elements of it and have Word apply the amendments automatically throughout the whole of the active document.

Generally, new documents you create in Word are based on the NORMAL.DOT template, and have the following pre-defined styles as a minimum:

- *Normal* – used for body text

- *Heading 1* – used for headings

- *Heading 2* – used for headings

- *Heading 3* – used for headings

Other templates have many more preset styles.

You can easily create (and apply) your own styles.

Finding out which text style is in force

Word provides a useful shortcut. If you're in any doubt about which style is associated with text, press Shift+F1. Now click in the text. This is the result:

Style details

Paragraph Formatting	
Paragraph Style: Indent: Left 0"	
Direct:	Centered, Border: Box (Single), Border Spacing: 1 pt
Font Formatting	
Paragraph Style: English (UK)	
Character Style:	
Direct:	Font: Britannic Bold, 72 pt, Expanded 3 pt

Press Esc to return to normal text editing.

Creating a text style

The easiest way to create a style is to:

1. apply the appropriate formatting enhancements to specific text and then select it

2. tell Word to save this formatting as a style

First, carry out step 1 above. Then pull down the Format menu and click Style. Now do the following:

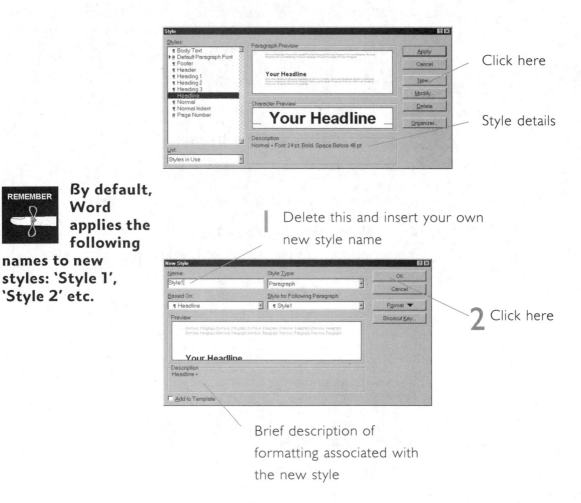

Click here

Style details

REMEMBER

By default, Word applies the following names to new styles: 'Style 1', 'Style 2' etc.

Delete this and insert your own new style name

2 Click here

Brief description of formatting associated with the new style

See 'Applying a text style' for how to use your new style.

Applying a text style

Word makes applying styles easy.

First, select the text you want to apply the style to. Or, if you only want to apply it to a single paragraph, place the insertion point inside it. Pull down the Format menu and click Style. Now do the following:

Click the style you want to apply

2 Click here

Style details

Shortcut for applying styles

Word makes it even easier to apply styles if you currently have the Formatting toolbar on-screen. (If you haven't, pull down the View menu and click Toolbars. In the Toolbars field within the Toolbars dialog, click Formatting. Click OK.)

Select the text you want to apply the style to. Then do the following:

Click here

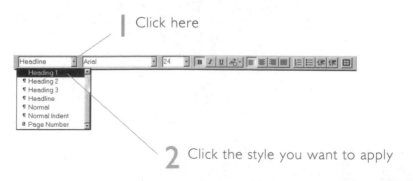

2 Click the style you want to apply

Amending a text style

The easiest way to modify an existing style is to:

1. apply the appropriate formatting enhancements to specific text and then select it

2. use the Formatting toolbar to tell Word to assign the selected formatting to the style

First, carry out step 1 above. Then do the following:

If the Formatting toolbar isn't currently visible, pull down the View menu and click Toolbars. In the Toolbars field within the Toolbars dialog, click Formatting. Click OK.

Click here

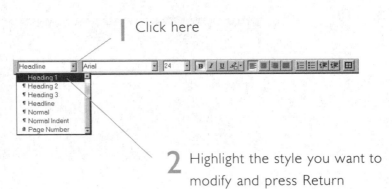

2 Highlight the style you want to modify and press Return

Word launches a special message. Do the following:

Make sure this is selected

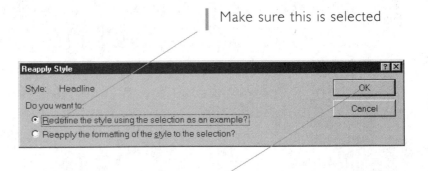

2 Click here to apply the specified amendments to the style

Deleting and viewing styles

Good housekeeping sometimes makes it necessary to remove unwanted styles from the active document. Word lets you do this very easily.

When you delete a style, any text associated with it automatically has the Normal style applied to it.

Another useful feature is the ability to make style names visible on the screen (but only within Normal view).

Deleting styles

Pull down the Format menu and click Style. Now carry out the following steps:

Click the style you want to remove

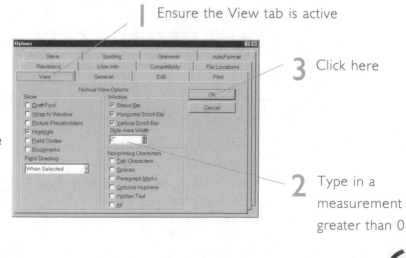

2 Click here

To enter Normal view, pull down the View menu and click Normal (if Normal already has a tick against it, you're already there).

Viewing style names

First, make sure you're in Normal view. Then pull down the Tools menu and click Options. Now do the following:

Ensure the View tab is active

3 Click here

Re step 2 - the figure you insert defines the extent of the 'Style Area', a zone on the left of the screen in which style names display.

2 Type in a measurement greater than 0

Spell-checking text (1)

Word lets you spell-check text in two ways:

- on-the-fly, as you type in text

- separately, after the text has been entered

Checking text on-the-fly

This is the default. When automatic spell-checking is in force, Word flags words it doesn't recognise with a red underline. If the word is wrong, right-click in it. Then do one of the following:

Word often provides a list of alternative suggestions. If one is correct, click it; Word replaces the flagged word with the correct version

If you want the flagged word to stand, click here

This is an experment in spell-checking. When Word encounters a s... ...ich isn't within its dictionary, it unde... ...red.

experiment
Ignore All
Add
Spelling...

Replaces this word by the selected suggestion

If the flagged word is correct, click here to add it to the dictionary

Disabling on-the-fly checking

Pull down the Tools menu and click Options. Activate the Spelling tab, then click Automatic Spell Checking (the cross disappears). Finally, click OK.

Spell-checking text (2)

Word makes use of two separate dictionaries. One can't be amended. However, the other - CUSTOM.DIC - can be thought of as yours. When you follow step 4 below, the flagged word is stored in CUSTOM.DIC and recognised in future checking sessions.

Checking text separately

To check all the text within the active document in one go, pull down the Tools menu and click Spelling. Word starts spell-checking the document from the beginning. When it encounters a word it doesn't recognise, Word flags it and produces a special dialog (see below). Usually, it provides alternative suggestions; if one of these is correct, you can opt to have it replace the flagged word. You can do this singly (i.e. just this instance is replaced) or globally (where all future instances – within the current checking session – are replaced).

Alternatively, you can have Word:

- ignore *this* instance of the flagged word and resume checking

- ignore *all* future instances of the word and resume checking

- add the word to CUSTOM.DIC and resume checking

Carry out step 1 below. Then follow step 2 or 3, or any one of steps 4, 5 or 6.

If the flagged word isn't correct and Word's suggestions are also wrong, type in the correct version in the Change To field. Then carry out step 2 or 3.

HANDY TIP

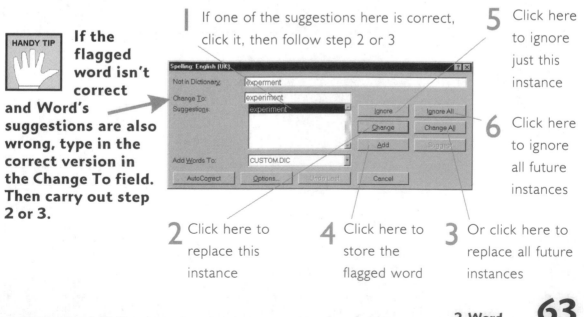

If one of the suggestions here is correct, click it, then follow step 2 or 3

5 Click here to ignore just this instance

6 Click here to ignore all future instances

2 Click here to replace this instance

4 Click here to store the flagged word

3 Or click here to replace all future instances

Searching for synonyms

Word lets you search for synonyms while you're editing the active document. You do this by calling up Word's resident thesaurus. The thesaurus categorises words into meanings, and each meaning is allocated various synonyms from which you can choose.

As a bonus, the thesaurus also supplies antonyms. For example, if you look up 'good' in the thesaurus, Word lists 'abominable', 'bad', 'base', 'corrupt' etc. as antonyms.

Using the thesaurus

First, select the word for which you require a synonym or antonym (or simply position the insertion point within it). Pull down the Tools menu and click Thesaurus. Now do the following:

The selected word appears here

Thesaurus: English {UK}		? X
Looked Up:	**Replace with Synonym:**	Replace
Good	moral	Look Up
Meanings:	moral	Cancel
moral (adj.)	upright	
skillful (adj.)	virtuous	
admirable (adj.)	righteous	Previous
obedient (adj.)	worthy	
kind (adj.)	exemplary	
worthy (adj.)	conscientious	
	blameless	

1 Click the appropriate meaning. Or click Antonyms, if appropriate

2 Click the synonym or antonym you want to replace the selected word

3 Click here to substitute the synonym or antonym for the selected word

Working with pictures

Word lets you add colour or greyscale pictures to the active document. Pictures – also called graphics – include:

- drawings produced in other programs

- clip art

- scanned photographs

Pictures are stored in various third-party formats. These formats are organised into two basic types:

Bitmap images

Bitmaps consist of pixels (dots) arranged in such a way that they form a graphic image. Because of the very nature of bitmaps, the question of 'resolution' – the sharpness of an image expressed in dpi (dots per inch) – is very important. Bitmaps look best if they're displayed at their correct resolution. Word can manipulate a wide variety of third-party bitmap graphics formats. These include: PCX, TIF, TGA and GIF.

Vector images

You can also insert vector graphics files into Word documents. Vector images consist of and are defined by algebraic equations. They're less complex than bitmaps: they contain less detail. Vector files can also include bitmap information.

Irrespective of the format type, Word can incorporate pictures with the help of special 'filters'. These are special mini-programs whose job it is to translate third-party formats into a form which Word can use. However, two supported formats do not require filters. These are:

- Windows Bitmap. A popular bitmap format. File suffix: BMP

- Windows Metafile. A frequently used vector format. Used for information exchange between just about all Windows programs. File suffix: WMF

Brief notes on picture formats

Graphics formats Word will accept include the following (the column on the left shows the relevant file suffix):

CGM — Computer Graphics Metafile. A vector format frequently used in the past, especially as a medium for clip-art transmission. Less often used nowadays.

EPS — Encapsulated PostScript. Perhaps the most widely used PostScript format. PostScript combines vector *and* bitmap data very successfully. Incorporates a low-resolution bitmap 'header' for preview purposes.

GIF — Graphics Interchange Format. Developed for the on-line transmission of graphics data across the CompuServe network. Just about any Windows program – and a lot more besides – will read GIF. Disadvantage: it can't handle more than 256 colours. Compression is supported.

PCD — (Kodak) PhotoCD. Used primarily to store photographs on CD.

PCX — An old standby. Originated with PC Paintbrush, a paint program. Used for years to transfer graphics data between Windows applications.

TGA — Targa. A high-end format, and also a bridge with so-called low-end computers (e.g. Amiga and Atari). Often used in PC and Mac paint and ray-tracing programs because of its high-resolution colour fidelity.

TIFF — Tagged Image File Format. Suffix: TIF. If anything, even more widely used than PCX, across a whole range of platforms and applications.

Inserting pictures

First, position the insertion point at the location within the active document where you want to insert the picture. Pull down the Insert menu and do the following:

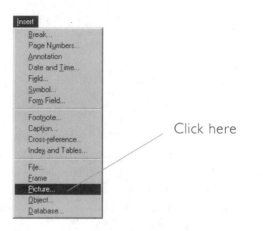

Click here

Now carry out the following steps:

2 Click here. In the drop-down list, click the drive/folder that hosts the picture

4 Click here

REMEMBER **Word provides a preview of what the picture will look like when it's been imported. See the Preview box on the right of the dialog.**

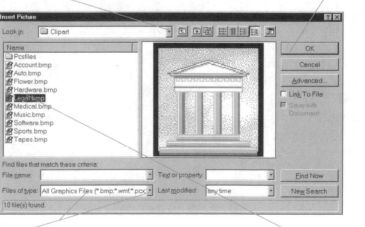

| Make sure All Graphics Files is shown. If it isn't, click the arrow and select it from the drop-down list

3 Click the picture file

Editing pictures

Once you've inserted pictures into a Word document, you can amend them in a variety of ways. For instance, you can:

- rescale them

- apply a border

- crop them

- move them

To carry out any of these operations, you have to select the relevant picture first. To do this, simply position the mouse pointer over the image and left-click once. Word surrounds the image with eight handles. These are positioned at the four corners, and midway on each side. The illustration below demonstrates these:

Handles

Users of the CD version of Office can find this picture - AIRCRAFT.JPG - within the VALUPAK folder.

Handles

Rescaling pictures

There are two ways in which you can rescale pictures:

- proportionally, where the height/width ratio remains constant

- disproportionately, where the height/width ratio is disrupted (this is sometimes called 'warping' or 'skewing')

To rescale a picture, first select it. Then move the mouse pointer over:

- one of the corner handles, if you want to rescale the image proportionately,

or

- one of the handles in the middle of the sides, if you want to warp it

In either eventuality, the mouse pointer changes to a double-headed arrow. Click and hold down the left mouse button. Drag outwards to increase the image size or inwards to decrease it. Release the mouse button to confirm the change.

Here, AIRCRAFT.JPG has been skewed from the right inwards

Bordering pictures

By default, Word does not apply a border to inserted pictures. However, you can apply a wide selection of borders if you want. You can specify:

- the type and thickness of the border

- how many sides the border should have

- the border colour

- whether the bordered picture should have a drop shadow

Applying a border

First, select the picture you want to border. Then pull down the Format menu and click Borders and Shading. Now do the following:

Re step 4 - click Shadow instead of Box if you want the border to have a drop shadow. Then proceed as normal.

1 Ensure the Borders tab is active

6 Click here

4 Click here to border all four sides of the image

2 Click the line type

Use step 5 to deselect the top, bottom, left or right picture borders. If you want to deselect more than one, repeat step 5 as often as necessary.

5 Click any of the picture sides to deselect the border

3 Click here; select the border colour from the drop-down list

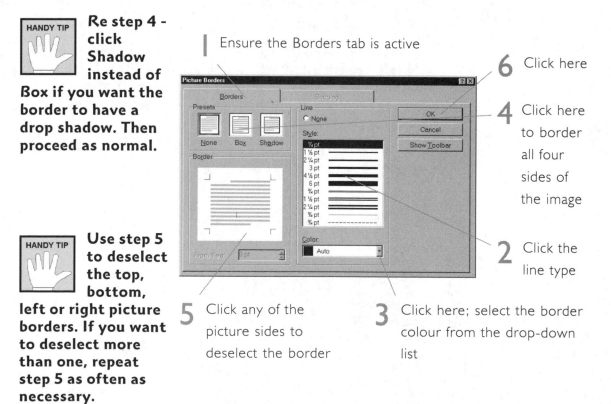

Cropping pictures

Cropping is the process of trimming the edges off a picture, either to make it fit within a smaller space or to remove parts that are unwanted.

Word provides two cropping methods.

Cropping with the mouse

First, select the picture you want to crop. Then press and hold down one Shift key. Move the mouse pointer over one of the available eight handles. Hold down the left mouse button and drag the handle inwards. Release the button to confirm the cropping operation.

Cropping from a dialog

This method lets you crop pictures with much more precision: you can specify the amount and direction of crop very accurately.

With the picture selected, pull down the Format menu and click Picture. Now do the following:

Type in crop measurements in any or all of the fields in this section

Picture		? X
Crop From	**Scaling**	OK
Left: 0"	Width: 100%	Cancel
Right: 0"	Height: 100%	Reset
Top: 0"	**Size**	Frame...
Bottom: 0"	Width: 0.92"	
	Height: 0.92"	
Original Size		
Width: 0.92"	Height: 0.92"	

2 Click here

Moving pictures

The easiest way to reposition a graphic on the page is to add a frame to it first.

A picture to which a frame has been added has a grey bounding box around it. It also has standard resizing handles:

To see frames, you must be using Page Layout view, or Print Preview.

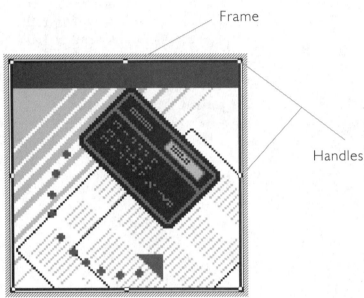

Frame

Handles

Frames adjust automatically to the size of the picture they contain. Additionally, text wraps around the frame, making it easier to position the picture effectively.

Inserting a frame and moving a picture

Select the picture in the normal way. Pull down the Insert menu and click Frame. Now place the mouse pointer anywhere inside or on the frame (but not on the handles). Click and hold down the left mouse button; drag the frame/picture to its new location.

Release the mouse button to confirm the move.

Page setup - an overview

You can control page layout to a great extent in Word. You can specify:

- the top, bottom, left and/or right page margins

- the distance between the top page edge and the top edge of the header

- the distance between the bottom page edge and bottom edge of the footer

The illustration below shows these page components:

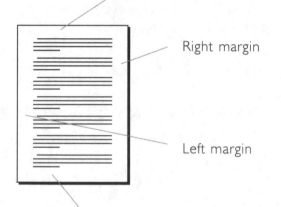

Top margin (including header)

Right margin

Left margin

Bottom margin (including footer)

You can also specify:

- the page size (irrespective of margins and headers/footers)

- the page orientation ('landscape' or 'portrait')

If none of the supplied page sizes is suitable, you can even customise your own.

Specifying margins

All documents have margins, because printing on the whole of a sheet is both unsightly and – in the case of many printers, since the mechanism has to grip the page – impossible. Documents need a certain amount of 'white space' (the unprinted portion of the page) to balance the areas which contain text and graphics. Without this, they can't be visually effective. As a result, it's important to set margins correctly.

Customising margins

First, position the insertion point at the location within the active document from which you want the new margin(s) to apply. Alternatively, select the relevant portion of your document. Then pull down the File menu and click Page Setup. Now carry out step 1 below. Then follow steps 2-5, as appropriate. Finally, carry out step 6.

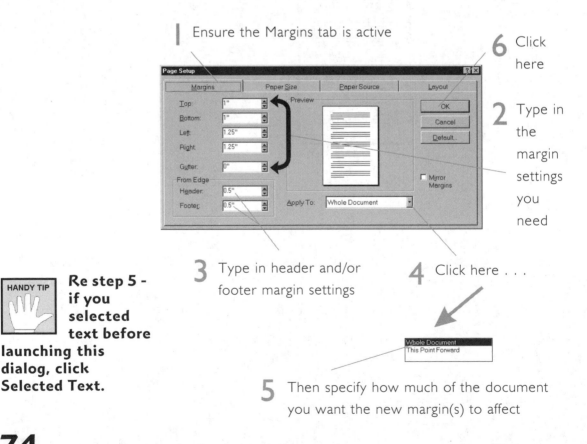

1 Ensure the Margins tab is active

6 Click here

2 Type in the margin settings you need

3 Type in header and/or footer margin settings

4 Click here . . .

5 Then specify how much of the document you want the new margin(s) to affect

Specifying the page size

Word comes with 11 preset page sizes – for instance, A4, A5 and Letter. These are suitable for most purposes. However, you can also set up your own page definition if you need to.

There are two aspects to every page size:

- a vertical measurement

- a horizontal measurement

Whatever the page size, you can have both portrait and landscape pages in the same document.

These can be varied according to orientation. There are two possible orientations:

Portrait   Landscape

To create your own page size, click Custom Size in step 2. Then type in height and width measurements in the Width & Height fields. Finally, carry out step 4.

Setting the page size

First, position the insertion point at the location within the active document from which you want the new margin(s) to apply. Then pull down the File menu and click Page Setup. Now do the following:

1 Ensure the Paper Size tab is active

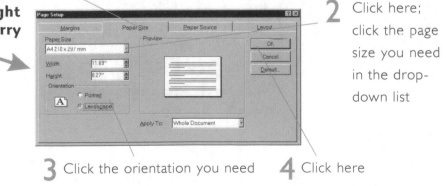

2 Click here; click the page size you need in the drop-down list

3 Click the orientation you need

4 Click here

Using Print Preview

Word provides a special view mode called Print Preview. This displays the active document exactly as it will look when printed. Use Print Preview as a final check just before you print your document.

You can customise the way Print Preview displays your document in various ways. For example, you can:

- zoom in or out on the active page

- specify how many pages display

- hide almost everything on screen apart from the document

Launching Print Preview

Pull down the File menu and click Print Preview. This is the result:

To leave Print Preview mode and return to either Normal or Page Layout view, simply press Esc.

Print Preview toolbar

Zooming in or out in Print Preview

There are two ways in which you can change the display magnification in Print Preview mode.

Using the mouse

To magnify *part* of the active document, click the Magnifier button in the Print Preview toolbar.

Click here

Right-click over a section of the Print Preview screen to decrease the magnification.

The mouse pointer changes to a magnifying class. Position this over the portion of the active document that you want to expand. Left-click once. Repeat this as often as necessary.

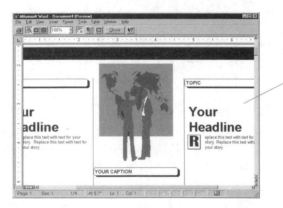

A magnified view of the upper central portion of the Print Preview screen

Using the Zoom Control button

To choose from pre-defined Zoom sizes, do the following:

Click here; select the preset Zoom size you need in the drop-down list

Multiple pages in Print Preview

In Print Preview mode, you can view as many as eighteen pages at the same time.

Turn to the Print Preview toolbar and do the following:

Click here

Word tells you here what page permutation you've chosen, e.g. '1 x 2' (2 pages displayed at full size), or '2 x 1' (2 pages displayed as thumbnails).

Word launches a graphical list:

Click and hold here . . .

Cancel

Position the mouse pointer over the first icon. Hold down the left mouse button. Drag the pointer to the right and/or down (the list expands as you do so). When you find the right page multiple, release the mouse button.

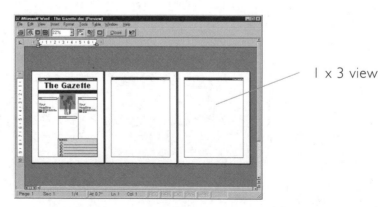

1 x 3 view

Clearing the screen in Print Preview

We saw earlier that it's possible to hide superfluous screen components in Normal and Page Layout views. You can also do this in Print Preview mode. Word calls this Full Screen view.

The advantage is that using Full Screen view in Print Preview mode makes more space available for display purposes. This is highly desirable unless you have a particularly large monitor. In Print Preview mode, Full Screen view hides all screen components with the exception of the Print Preview toolbar and the horizontal and vertical rulers.

Implementing Full Screen view

Refer to the Print Screen toolbar and do the following:

Click here

HANDY TIP **There is a keyboard shortcut you can use to leave Full Screen view: simply press Esc.**

To leave Full Screen view, repeat this procedure.

1 x 3 pages in Full Screen view

Printer setup

Most Word documents need to be printed eventually. Before you can begin printing, however, you need to ensure that:

The question of which printer you select affects how the document displays in Print Preview mode.

- the correct printer is selected (if you have more than one installed)

- the correct printer settings are in force

Word calls these collectively the 'printer setup'.

Irrespective of the printer selected, the settings vary in accordance with the job in hand. For example, most printer drivers (the software which 'drives' the printer) allow you to specify whether or not you want pictures printed. Additionally, they often allow you to specify the resolution or print quality of the output . . .

Selecting the printer and/or settings

At any time before you're ready to print a document, pull down the File menu and click Print. Now do the following:

Click here; select the printer you want from the list

This procedure can also be followed from within Print Preview mode.

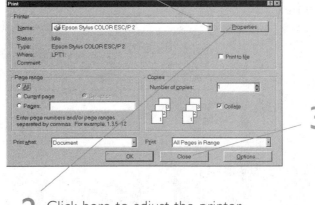

3 Click here

2 Click here to adjust the printer settings (for how to do this, see your printer's manual)

Printing - an overview

Once the active document is how you want it (and you've customised the printer setup appropriately), you'll probably need to print it out. Word makes this process easy and straightforward. It lets you set a variety of options before you do so.

Alternatively, you can simply opt to print your document with the default options in force (Word provides a 'fast track' approach to this).

Available print options include:

•   the number of copies you want printed

•   whether you want the copies 'collated'. This is the process whereby Word prints one full copy at a time. For instance, if you're printing three copies of a 40-page document, Word prints pages 1-40 of the first document, followed by pages 1-40 of the second and pages 1-40 of the third.

•   which pages (or page ranges) you want printed

•   whether you want to limit the print run to odd or even pages

•   whether you want the print run restricted to text you selected before initiating printing

•   whether you want the pages printed in reverse order (e.g. from the last page to the first)

•   the quality of the eventual output (with many printers, Word allows you to print with minimal formatting for proofing purposes)

•   whether you want to go on working in Word while the document prints (the default). Word calls this 'background printing'.

You can 'mix and match' these, as appropriate.

Printing - the fast track approach

Since documents and printing needs vary dramatically, it's often necessary to customise print options before you begin printing.

For example, if you've created a document which contains numerous pictures, you may well want to print out a draft copy for proofing purposes prior to printing the final version (although Print Preview mode provides a very effective indication of how a document will look when printed, there are still errors which are only detectable when you're working with hard copy). In this situation, you may wish to exclude pictures or print with minimal formatting. (For how to set your own print options, see 'Customised printing (1)' and 'Customised printing (2)'.)

On the other hand, simple documents can often benefit from a simple approach. In this case, you may well be content to print using the default options. Word recognises this and provides a method which bypasses the standard Print dialog, and is therefore much quicker and easier to use.

Printing with the current print options

First, ensure your printer is ready. Make sure the Standard toolbar is visible. (If it isn't, pull down the View menu and click Toolbars. In the Toolbars section of the Toolbars dialog, click Standard. Then click OK.) Now do the following:

Click here

Word starts printing the active document immediately.

Customised printing (1)

If you need to set revised print options before printing, do the following.

Pull down the File menu and click Print. Now carry out steps 1-5, as appropriate. Finally, carry out step 6.

If you need to print in reverse order or with minimal formatting (or if you want to turn off background printing), follow the procedures under 'Customised printing (2)' before you carry out step 6 here.

1 Click here to deselect collation

2 Type in the number of copies

HANDY TIP

Re step 3 - separate non-adjacent pages with commas but no spaces - e.g. to print pages 5, 12, 16 & 19 type in: '5,12,16,19'. Enter contiguous pages with dashes - e.g. to print pages 12 to 23 inclusive, type in: '12-23'. (Omit the quote marks.)

3 Type in the relevant page range (see tip opposite)

4 Click here if you selected text before launching this dialog and this is all you want to print

6 Click here

5 To print only odd or even pages, click here; select Odd Pages or Even Pages

Word starts printing the active document.

Customised printing (2)

Other print options are accessible from within a special dialog. This is launched from within the Print dialog.

First, pull down the File menu and click Print. Then do the following:

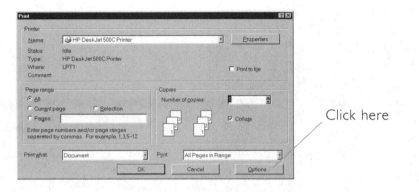

Click here

Now carry out steps 1-3 below, as appropriate. Then follow step 4.

Click here to print with minimal formatting

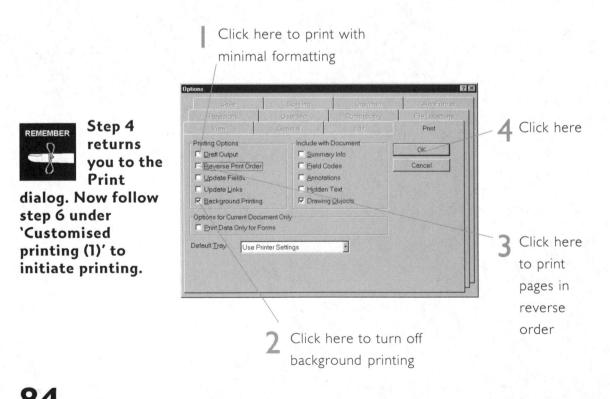

REMEMBER

Step 4 returns you to the Print dialog. Now follow step 6 under 'Customised printing (1)' to initiate printing.

4 Click here

3 Click here to print pages in reverse order

2 Click here to turn off background printing

SECTION THREE

Excel

This chapter gives you the fundamentals of using Excel. You'll learn how to work with data and formulas, and how to move around through worksheets. You'll also learn how to insert pictures, and make your data more visually effective. Finally, you'll customise page layout/printing.

Covers

The Excel screen

Below is a detailed illustration of the Excel screen.

Title bar   Menu bar   Column letters

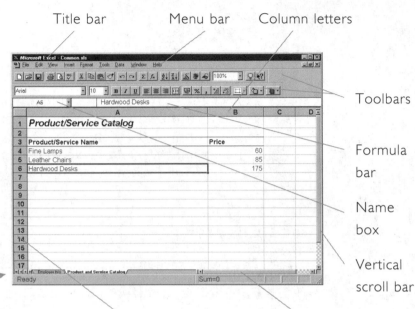

Toolbars

Formula bar

Name box

Vertical scroll bar

Row numbers   Horizontal scroll bar

This is the worksheet tab area. The screen components here are used to move through Excel documents.

Some of these screen components can be hidden at will.

Specifying which screen components display

Pull down the Tools menu and click Options. Then:

Ensure the View tab is active

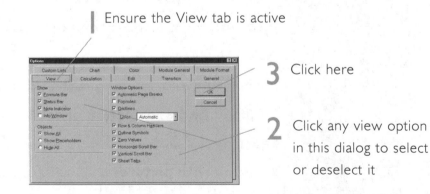

3 Click here

2 Click any view option in this dialog to select or deselect it

Entering data (1)

When you start Excel, you're presented with a new blank spreadsheet:

When you run Excel, you're actually opening a new workbook (see below). Excel calls these 'Book 1', 'Book 2' etc.

Cells

This means that you can start entering data immediately.

In Excel, you can enter the following basic data types:

- values (i.e. numbers)

- text (e.g. headings and explanatory material)

- functions (e.g. Sine or Cosine)

- formulas (combinations of values, text and functions)

Columns are vertical, rows horizontal. Each worksheet can have as many as 256 columns and 16,384 rows, making a grand total of 4,194,304 cells.

You enter data into 'cells'. Cells are formed where rows and columns intersect. In the figure above, cells H6 and G8 are flagged for illustration purposes.

Collections of rows/columns and cells are known in Excel as worksheets. Worksheets are organised into workbooks (by default, each workbook has 16 worksheets). Workbooks are the files that are stored on disk when you save your work in Excel.

Entering data (2)

Although you can enter data *directly* into a cell (by simply clicking in the cell and typing it in), there's another method you can use which is often easier. Excel provides a special screen component known as the Formula bar.

The illustration below shows the end of a blank worksheet. Some sample text has been inserted into cell IV16384 (note that the Name box tells you which cell is currently active).

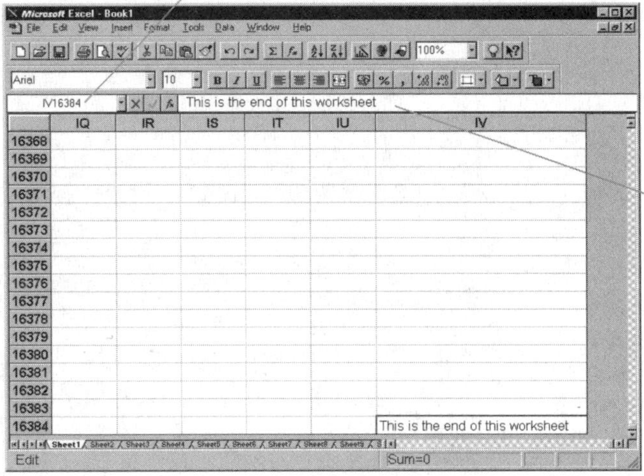

Name box

Formula bar

Entering data via the Formula bar

Click the cell you want to insert data into. Then click the Formula bar. Type in the data. Then follow step 1 below. If you decide not to proceed with the operation, follow step 2 instead:

HANDY TIP **You can use a keyboard route to confirm operations in the Formula bar: simply press Return.**

Click here

This is the end of this worksheet

2 Click here to cancel the operation

Modifying existing data

You can amend the contents of a cell in two ways:

- via the Formula bar

- from within the cell

When you use either of these methods, Excel enters a special state known as Edit Mode.

Amending existing data using the Formula bar

Click the cell whose contents you want to change. Then click in the Formula bar. Make the appropriate revisions and/or additions. Then press Return. Excel updates the relevant cell.

Amending existing data internally

Click the cell whose contents you want to change. Press F2. Make the appropriate revisions and/or additions *within the cell*. Then press Return.

The illustration below shows a section of a sample workbook – COMMON.XLS – supplied with Excel.

A magnified view of cell B4, in Edit Mode

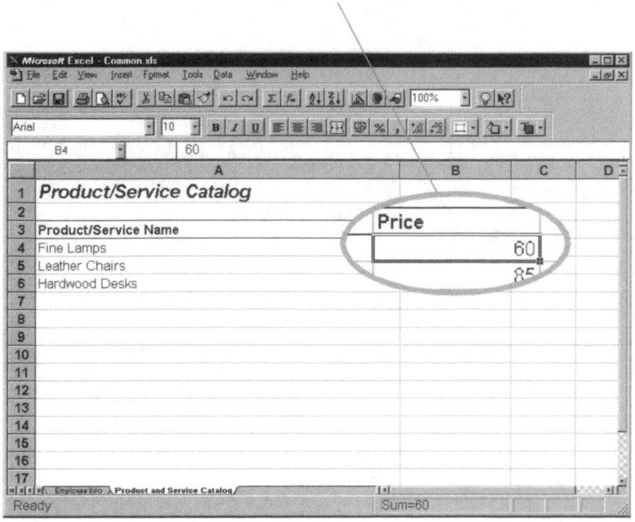

Working with cell ranges

When you're working with more than one cell, it's often convenient and useful to organise them in 'ranges'.

A range is a rectangular arrangement of cells. In the illustration below, cells A3, A4, A5, A6, B3, B4, B5 and B6 have been selected.

A selected cell range

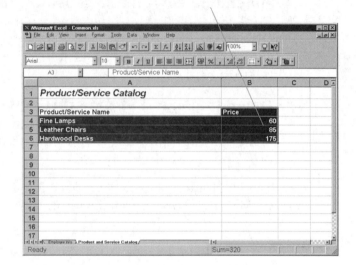

The above description of the relevant cells is very cumbersome. It's much more useful to use a form of shorthand. Excel (using the start and end cells as reference points) refers to these cells as:

A3:B6

You can extend this even more. Cell addresses can also incorporate a component which refers to the worksheet that contains the range. For example, to denote that the range A3:B6 is in worksheet 8, you'd use:

Sheet8!A3:B6

Moving around in worksheets (1)

Excel worksheets are huge. Moving to cells which happen to be visible is easy: you simply click in the relevant cell. However, Excel provides several techniques you can use to jump to less accessible areas.

Using the scroll bars

Use any of the following methods:

1. to scroll quickly to another section of the active worksheet, drag the scroll box along the scroll bar until you reach it

2. to move one window to the right or left, click to the left or right of the scroll box in the horizontal scroll bar

3. to move one window up or down, click above or below the scroll box in the vertical scroll bar

4. to move up or down by one row, click the arrows in the vertical scroll bar

5. to move left or right by one column, click the arrows in the horizontal scroll bar

Scroll boxes

Scroll arrows

Scroll arrows

Moving around in worksheets (2)

Using the keyboard
You can use the following techniques:

1.　use the cursor keys to move one cell left, right, up or down.

2.　hold down Ctrl as you use 1. above; this jumps to the edge of the current section (e.g. if cell B11 is active and you hold down Ctrl as you press →, Excel jumps to IV11, the last cell in row 11).

3.　press Home to jump to the first cell in the active row, or Ctrl+Home to move to A1.

4.　press Page Up or Page Down to move up or down by one screen.

5.　press Alt+Page Down to move one screen to the right, or Alt+Page Up to move one screen to the left.

You can use a keyboard shortcut to launch the Go To dialog: simply press F5, or Ctrl+G.

Using the Go To dialog
Excel provides a special dialog which you can use to specify precise cell destinations.

Pull down the Edit menu and click Go To. Now do the following:

Re step 1 - a cell's 'reference' (or 'address') identifies it in relation to its position in a worksheet, e.g. B11 or H23. You can also type in cell ranges here.

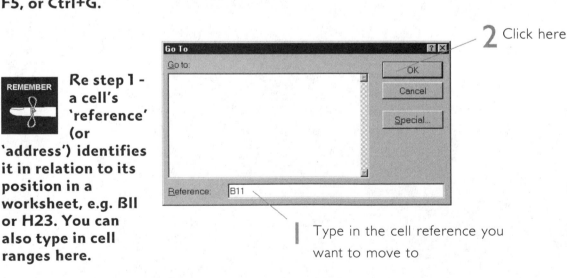

2 Click here

Type in the cell reference you want to move to

Switching between worksheets

Because workbooks have more than one worksheet, Excel provides two easy and convenient methods for moving between them.

Using the Tab area
You can use the Tab area (at the base of the Excel screen) to:

• jump to the first or last sheet

• jump to the next or previous sheet

• jump to a specific sheet

See the illustration below:

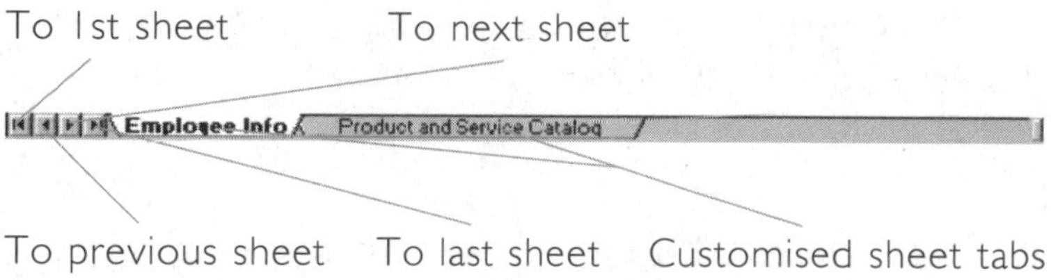

To 1st sheet   To next sheet

`|◄| ◄| ►| ►|\ Employee Info / Product and Service Catalog /`

To previous sheet   To last sheet   Customised sheet tabs

To move to a specific sheet, simply click the relevant tab.

An example: in the illustration above, to jump to the Product and Service Catalog worksheet, simply click the appropriate tab.

When you click a worksheet tab, Excel emboldens the name and makes the tab background white.

Using the keyboard
You can use a keyboard shortcut here.

Press Ctrl+Page Up to move to the previous tab, or Ctrl+Page Down to move to the next.

Other operations on worksheets (1)

We said earlier that, by default, each workbook has 16 worksheets. However, you can easily:

- add new worksheets

- delete existing worksheets

- move existing worksheets

Inserting a single worksheet

In the worksheet tab area at the base of the screen, click the tab which represents the sheet in front of which you want the new worksheet inserted. Pull down the Insert menu and click Worksheet.

HANDY TIP

You can use a keyboard shortcut to insert a worksheet: simply press Shift+F11.

Inserting more than one worksheet

To add multiple worksheets, hold down one Shift key as you click the required number of sheet tabs (in other words, to add 6 new worksheets, shift-click 6 tabs). Then pull down the Insert menu and click Worksheet.

Deleting worksheets

In the worksheet tab area, click a single worksheet tab (or shift-click multiple tabs to delete more than one worksheet at a time). Pull down the Edit menu and click Delete Sheet. Excel launches a special message. Do the following:

BEWARE

When you delete a worksheet, you automatically erase the worksheet contents, too.

Click here to proceed
with the deletion

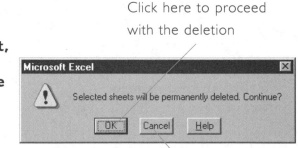

Microsoft Excel

Selected sheets will be permanently deleted. Continue?

OK   Cancel   Help

Or here to cancel it and
return to your workbook

Other operations on worksheets (2)

You can perform two kinds of move operation on worksheets. You can:

- rearrange the worksheet order within a given workbook

- transfer a worksheet to another workbook

Rearranging worksheets

To select a single worksheet, click the relevant sheet tab in the worksheet tab area. Or select more than one worksheet by holding down one Shift key as you click multiple tabs. With the mouse pointer still over the selected tab(s), hold down the left mouse button and drag them to their new location. Release the mouse button to confirm the operation.

Moving worksheets to another workbook

To select a single worksheet, click the relevant sheet tab in the worksheet tab area. Or select more than one worksheet by holding down one Shift key as you click multiple tabs. Pull down the Edit menu and click Move or Copy Sheet. Now do the following:

1 Click here; select the new host workbook from the drop-down list

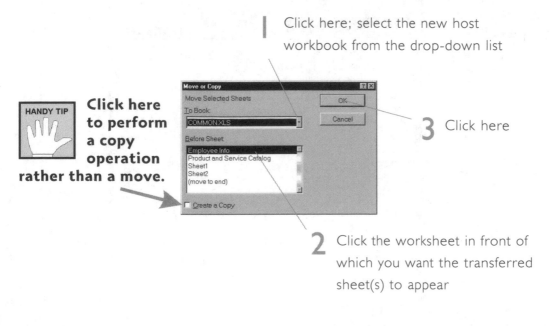

HANDY TIP

Click here to perform a copy operation rather than a move.

3 Click here

2 Click the worksheet in front of which you want the transferred sheet(s) to appear

Selection techniques (1)

With the exception of the first cell, a selected range is filled with black.

HANDY TIP

You can use another keyboard route. Place the cell pointer in the first cell. Press F8. Use the cursor keys to define the selection. Finally, press F8 again.

Before you can carry out any editing operations on cells in Excel, you have to select them first. Selecting a single cell is very easy: you merely click in it. However, Excel provides a variety of selection techniques which you can use to select more than one cell.

Selecting adjacent cell ranges

The easiest way to do this is to use the mouse. Click in the first cell in the range; hold down the left mouse button and drag over the remaining cells. Release the mouse button.

You can use the keyboard, too. Position the cell pointer over the first cell in the range. Hold down one Shift key as you use the relevant cursor key to extend the selection. Release the keys when the correct selection has been defined.

Selecting separate cell ranges

Excel lets you select more than one range at a time. Look at the illustration below:

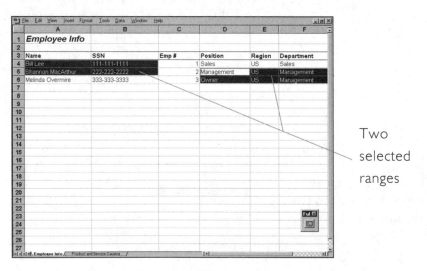

Two selected ranges

To select joint ranges, select the first in the normal way (you can't use the 'F8' method here). Then hold down Ctrl as you select subsequent ranges.

Selection techniques (2)

Selecting a single row or column

To select every cell within a row or column automatically, click on the row or column heading.

Column heading

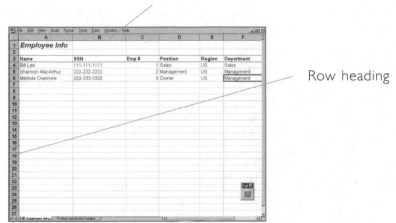

Row heading

Selecting multiple rows or columns

To select more than one row or column, click on the row or column heading. Hold down the left mouse button and drag to select adjacent rows or columns.

Selecting an entire worksheet

Click the Select All button:

A magnified view of the Select All button

HANDY TIP **You can use a keyboard shortcut** to select every cell automatically: simply press Ctrl+A.

Formulas - an overview

Formulas are cell entries which define how other values relate to each other.

As a very simple example, consider the following:

This is the sample workbook supplied with Excel. An extra cell has been defined which returns the total of cells B4:B6. Obviously, in this instance you could insert the total easily enough yourself because the individual values are so small, and because we're only dealing with a small number of cells. But what happens if the cell values are larger and/or more numerous, or – more to the point – if they're liable to change frequently?

The answer is to insert a formula which carries out the necessary calculation automatically.

If you look at the Formula bar in the illustration, you'll see the formula which does this:

=SUM(B4:B6)

Many Excel formulas are much more complex than this, but the principles remain the same.

Inserting a formula

Arguments (e.g. cell references) relating to functions are always contained in brackets.

All formulas in Excel begin with an equals sign. This is usually followed by a permutation of the following:

- an operand (cell reference, e.g. B4)

- a function (e.g. the summation function, SUM)

- an arithmetical operator (+, −, / and *)

- comparison operators (<, >, <=, >= and =)

Excel supports a very wide range of functions organised into numerous categories. For more information on how to insert functions, see Using the Function Wizard.

The mathematical operators are (in the order in which they appear in the bulleted list): *plus*, *minus*, *divide* and *multiply*.

The comparison operators are (in the order in which they appear in the list): *less than*, *greater than*, *less than or equal to*, *greater than or equal to* and *equals*.

There are two ways to enter formulas:

Entering a formula directly into the cell
Click the cell in which you want to insert a formula. Then type =, followed by your formula. When you've finished, press Return.

Entering a formula into the Formula bar
This is usually the most convenient method.

Click the cell in which you want to insert a formula. Then click in the Formula bar. Type =, followed by your formula. When you've finished, press Return or do the following:

Click here

Using the Function Wizard

Functions are pre-defined tools which accomplish specific tasks. These tasks are often calculations; occasionally, however, they're more generalised (e.g. some functions simply return dates and/or times). In effect, functions replace one or more formulas.

Excel provides a special Wizard to help ensure that you enter functions correctly. This is useful for the following reasons:

Excel organises its functions under convenient headings (e.g. Financial, Date & Time, Statistical and Text).

HANDY TIP

- Excel provides so many functions, it's convenient to apply them from a centralised source

- the Function Wizard ensures the functions are entered with the correct syntax

Functions can only be used in formulas.

Inserting a function with the Function Wizard

At the relevant juncture during the process of inserting a formula, pull down the Insert menu and click Function. Now do the following:

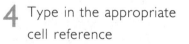

1 Click the function heading

2 Click the function you want to use

3 Click here

REMEMBER

Re step 4 - repeat this as many times as required for successive fields. As you do so, Excel adds additional fields to the dialog.

Now do the following (this dialog varies with the function):

4 Type in the appropriate cell reference

5 Click here to insert the function

Amending row/column sizes

Sooner or later, you'll find it necessary to change the width of rows or columns. This necessity arises when there is too much data in cells to display adequately. You can enlarge or shrink single or multiple rows/columns.

Changing row height

To change one row's height, click the row heading. If you want to change multiple rows, hold down Ctrl and click the appropriate extra headings. Then place the mouse pointer over the line located just under the row heading(s). Hold down the left mouse button and drag the line up or down to decrease or increase the row(s) respectively. Release the mouse button to confirm the operation.

HANDY TIP

Excel has a useful 'best fit' feature. Simply double-click the line below the selected row headings, or to the right of selected column headings, to have the rows or columns adjust themselves automatically to their contents.

A magnified view of the line to drag if you're amending rows 4, 5 and 6 jointly

Changing column widths

To change one column's width, click the column heading. If you want to change multiple columns, hold down Ctrl and click the appropriate extra headings. Then place the mouse pointer over the line located just to the right of the column heading(s). Hold down the left mouse button and drag the line right or left to widen or narrow the column(s) respectively. Release the mouse button to confirm the operation.

Inserting cells, rows or columns

You can insert additional cells, rows or columns into worksheets.

Inserting a new row or column

First, select one or more cells within the row(s) or column(s) where you want to carry out the insert operation. Now pull down the Insert menu and click Row or Column, as appropriate. Excel inserts the new row(s) or column(s) immediately.

If you select cells in more than one row or column, Excel inserts the equivalent number of new rows or columns.

	A	B
1	*Product/Service Catalog*	
2		
3	Product/Service Name	Price
4	Fine Lamps	60
5	Leather Chairs	85
6	Hardwood Desks	175
7		
8	Total	320
9		
10		
11		

An extract of a worksheet. Here, one new column or two new rows are being added

Inserting a new cell range

Select the range where you want to insert the new cells. Pull down the Insert menu and click Cells. Now carry out step 1 or step 2 below. Finally, follow step 3.

| Click here to have Excel make room for the new cells by moving the selected range *to the right*

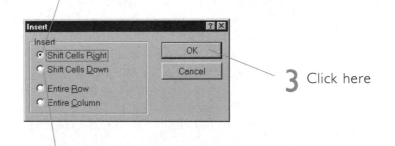

3 Click here

2 Click here to have Excel make room for the new cells by moving the selected range *down*

AutoFill

Excel lets you insert data series automatically. This is a very useful and time-saving feature. Look at the illustration below:

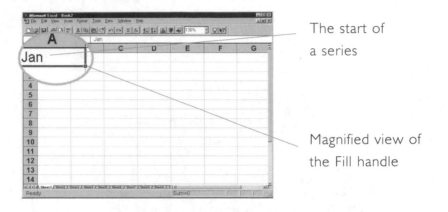

The start of a series

Magnified view of the Fill handle

If you wanted to insert month names in successive cells in column A, you could do so manually. But there's a much easier way. You can use Excel's AutoFill feature.

Using AutoFill to create a series

Type in the first element(s) of the series in consecutive cells. Select the cells. Then position the mouse pointer over the Fill handle in the bottom right-hand corner of the last cell (the pointer changes to a crosshair). Hold down the left mouse button and drag the handle over the cells into which you want to extend the series (in the example here, over A2:A12). When you release the mouse button, Excel extrapolates the initial entry or entries into the appropriate series.

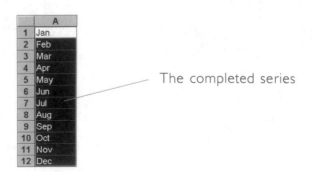

The completed series

Changing number formats

Excel lets you apply formatting enhancements to cells and their contents. You can:

- specify a number format

- customise the font, typesize and style of contents

- specify cell alignment

- border and/or shade cells

Specifying a number format

You can customise the way cell contents (e.g. numbers and dates/times) display in Excel. For example, you can specify at what point numbers are rounded up. Available formats are organised under several general categories. These include: Number, Accounting and Fraction.

Select the cells whose contents you want to customise. Pull down the Format menu and click Cells. Now do the following:

Ensure the Number tab is active

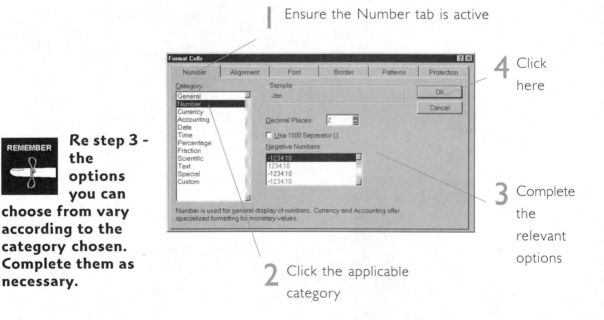

4 Click here

3 Complete the relevant options

REMEMBER

Re step 3 - the options you can choose from vary according to the category chosen. Complete them as necessary.

2 Click the applicable category

Changing fonts and styles

Excel lets you carry out the following actions on cell contents (numbers and/or text):

- apply a new font and/or typesize

- apply a font style (for most fonts, you can choose from: Regular, Italic, Bold or Bold Italic)

- apply a colour

- apply a special effect (<u>underlining</u>, ~~strikethrough~~, superscript or subscript)

Amending the appearance of cell contents

Select the cell(s) whose contents you want to reformat. Pull down the Format menu and click Cells. Carry out step 1 below. Now follow any of steps 2-5, as appropriate, or either or both of the two tips. Finally, carry out step 6.

HANDY TIP

To underline the specified contents, click here, and then click the type of underlining you want to apply.

Ensure the Font tab is active

3 Type in the typesize you need

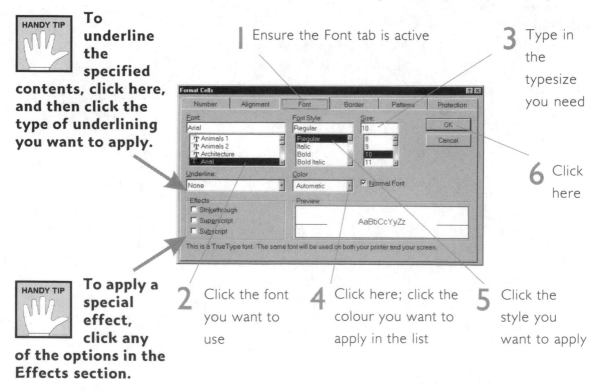

6 Click here

HANDY TIP

To apply a special effect, click any of the options in the Effects section.

2 Click the font you want to use

4 Click here; click the colour you want to apply in the list

5 Click the style you want to apply

Cell alignment (1)

By default, Excel aligns text to the left of cells, and numbers to the right. However, if you want you can change this.

You can specify alignment under two broad headings: Horizontal and Vertical.

Horizontal alignment

The main options are:

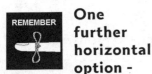

One further horizontal option - Center across selection - centres cell contents across more than one cell (if you selected a cell range before initiating it).

General   the default (see above)

Left   contents are aligned from the left

Center   contents are centred

Right   contents are aligned from the right

Fill   contents are duplicated so that they fill the cell

Justify   a combination of Left and Right.

Vertical alignment

Available options are:

Top   cell contents align with the top of the cell(s)

Center   contents are centred

Bottom   contents align with the cell bottom

Justify   contents are aligned along the top and bottom of the cell(s)

Most of these settings parallel features found in Word (and many other word-processors). The difference, however, lies in the fact that Excel has to align data within the bounds of cells rather than a page. When it aligns text, it often needs to employ its own version of text wrap. See 'Cell alignment (2)' for more information on this.

Cell alignment (2)

Other alignment features you can set are orientation and text wrap.

Orientation controls the direction of text flow within cells; there are four available options. These are expressed visually in the Orientation field in the Format Cells dialog.

When the Wrap Text option is selected, Excel – instead of overflowing any surplus text into adjacent cells to the right – forces it onto separate lines within the host cell.

	A	B	C
1	Here, text wrap is not in force		
2			
3			
4			
5	This text, however, *has* been wrapped		

— Text wrap in action

Customising cell alignment

Select the cell(s) whose contents you want to realign. Pull down the Format menu and click Cells. Carry out step 1 below. Now follow any or all of steps 2-5, as appropriate. Finally, carry out step 6.

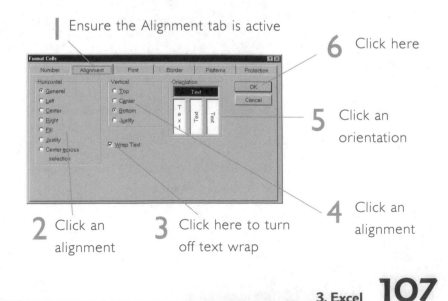

Ensure the Alignment tab is active

6 Click here

5 Click an orientation

4 Click an alignment

2 Click an alignment

3 Click here to turn off text wrap

Bordering cells

Excel lets you define a border around:

- the perimeter of a selected cell range

- the individual cells within a selected cell range

- specific sides within a cell range

You can customise the border by choosing from a selection of pre-defined border styles. You can also colour the border, if required.

Applying a cell border

First, select the cell range you want to border. Pull down the Format menu and click Cells. Now carry out steps 1 and 2 below. Step 3 is optional. Finally, follow steps 4 and 5. If you're setting multiple border options, repeat steps 2-4 as required.

HANDY TIP **Re step 4 – Outline borders the perimeter of the selected cells. The other options (you can click more than 1) affect individual sides.**

1 Ensure the Border tab is active

2 Click the relevant border style option

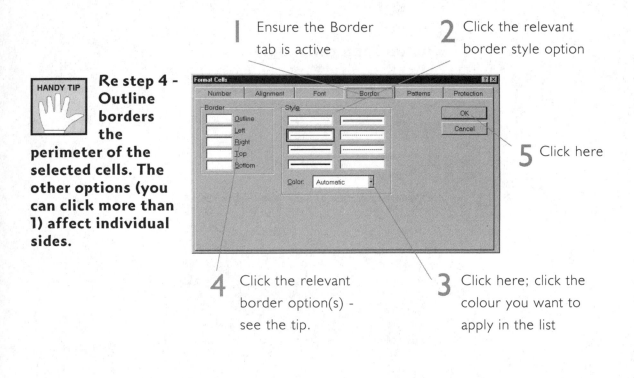

5 Click here

4 Click the relevant border option(s) - see the tip.

3 Click here; click the colour you want to apply in the list

Shading cells

Excel lets you apply the following to cells:

- a pattern

- a pattern colour

- a background colour

You can do any of these singly, or in combination.
Interesting effects can be achieved by using pattern colours
with coloured backgrounds.

Applying a pattern or background

First, select the cell range you want to shade. Pull down the
Format menu and click Cells. Now carry out steps 1 and 2
below. Step 3 is optional. Finally, follow steps 4 and 5. If
you're setting multiple border options, repeat steps 2-4 as
required.

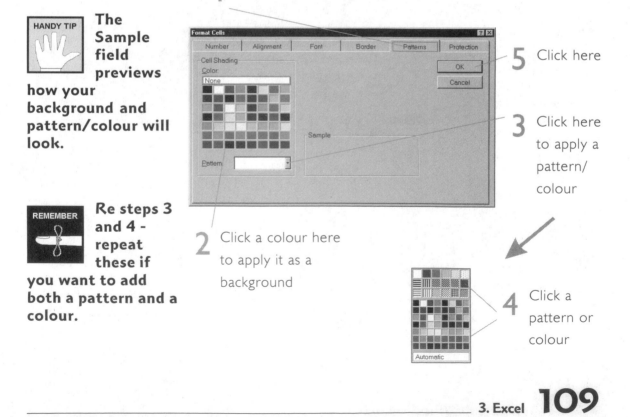

Ensure the Patterns tab is active

The Sample field previews how your background and pattern/colour will look.

5 Click here

3 Click here to apply a pattern/ colour

Re steps 3 and 4 - repeat these if you want to add both a pattern and a colour.

2 Click a colour here to apply it as a background

4 Click a pattern or colour

AutoFormat

Excel provides a shortcut to the formatting of worksheet data: AutoFormat.

AutoFormat consists of 16 pre-defined formatting schemes. These incorporate specific excerpts from the font, number, alignment, border and shading options discussed earlier. You can apply any of these schemes (and their associated formatting) to selected cell ranges with just a few mouse clicks. You can even specify which scheme elements you *don't* wish to use.

AutoFormat works with most arrangements of worksheet data.

Using AutoFormat

First, select the cell range you want to apply an automatic format to. Pull down the Format menu and click AutoFormat. Now carry out step 1 below. Steps 2 and 3 are optional. Finally, follow step 4.

HANDY TIP **The Sample field previews how your data will look with the specified AutoFormat.**

REMEMBER **Re step 3 - the dialog shown here is an addition to the AutoFormat dialog.**

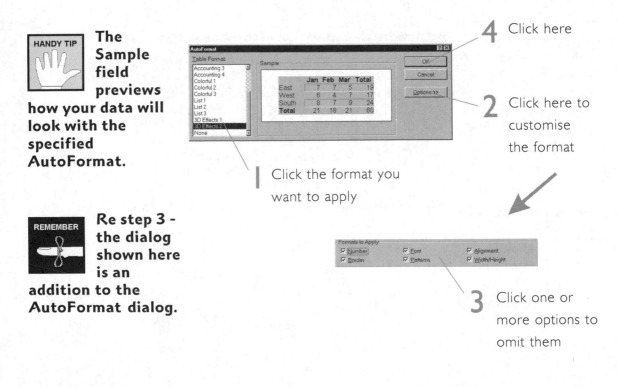

4 Click here

2 Click here to customise the format

Click the format you want to apply

3 Click one or more options to omit them

Find operations

Excel lets you search for and jump to text or numbers (in short, any information) in your worksheets. This is a particularly useful feature when worksheets become large and complex.

You can organise your search by rows or by columns. You can also specify whether Excel looks in:

•   cells that contain formulas

•   cells that don't contain formulas

Additionally, you can insist that Excel only flag exact matches (i.e. if you searched for '11', Excel would not find '1111'), and you can also limit text searches to text which has the case you specified (e.g. searching for 'PRODUCT LIST' would not find 'Product List').

To search for data over more than one worksheet, select the relevant sheet tabs before following steps 1-6.

Searching for data

Place the mouse pointer at the location in the active worksheet from which you want the search to begin. Pull down the Edit menu and click Find. Now carry out step 1 below, then any of steps 2-5. Finally, carry out step 6.

If you want to restrict the search to specific cells, select a cell range before you follow steps 1-6.

1 Type in the data you want to find

4 Click here for a case-specific search

6 Click here

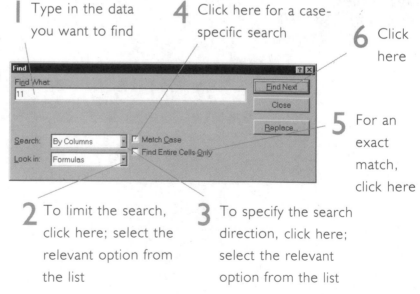

5 For an exact match, click here

2 To limit the search, click here; select the relevant option from the list

3 To specify the search direction, click here; select the relevant option from the list

Find-and-replace operations

When you search for data, you can also – if you want – have Excel replace it with something else.

Find-and-replace operations can be organised by rows or by columns. However, unlike straight searches, you can't specify whether Excel looks in cells that contain formulas or those that don't. As with straight searches, you can, however, limit find-and-replace operations to exact matches and also (in the case of text) to precise case matches.

Normally, find-and-replace operations only affect the worksheet in which they're conducted. If you want to carry out an operation over multiple worksheets, see the tip.

Running a find-and-replace operation

Place the mouse pointer at the location in the active worksheet from which you want the search to begin (or select a cell range if you want to restrict the find-and-replace operation to this). Pull down the Edit menu and click Replace. Now carry out step 1 below, then any of steps 2-5. Finally, carry out step 6, and steps 7 and/or 8 as required.

HANDY TIP

To search for and replace data over more than one worksheet, select the relevant sheet tabs before following steps 1-8.

1 Type in the data you want to find

4 Click here for a case-specific search

6 Click here to find the 1st occurrence

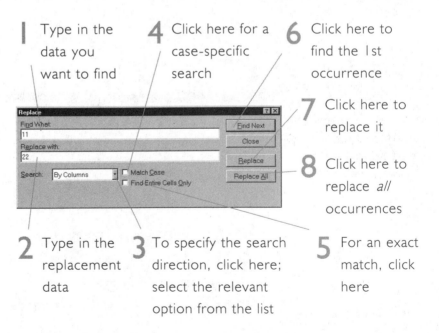

7 Click here to replace it

8 Click here to replace *all* occurrences

2 Type in the replacement data

3 To specify the search direction, click here; select the relevant option from the list

5 For an exact match, click here

Charting - an overview

Excel has comprehensive charting capabilities. You can have it convert selected data into its visual equivalent. To do this, Excel offers a wide number of chart formats and sub-formats.

You can create a chart:

- as a picture within the parent worksheet

- as a separate chart sheet

Chart sheets have their own tabs in the tab area; these operate just like worksheet tabs.

Excel uses a special Wizard – ChartWizard – to make the process of creating charts as easy and convenient as possible.

The illustration below is a sample chart based on the data within COMMON.XLS, the workbook supplied with Excel:

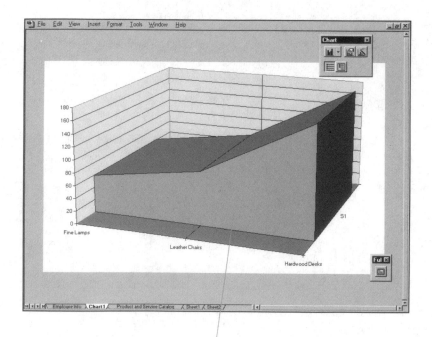

A 3-D Area chart

Creating an embedded chart

When you select the data cells, include a row or column of text entries if you want these inserted into the chart as descriptive labels.

First, select the cells you want converted into a chart. Pull down the Insert menu and click Chart, followed by On This Sheet. The cursor becomes a crosshair. Move this to the location where you want the chart to begin. Hold down the left mouse button and drag to define the chart area. (Hold down one Shift key as you drag if you want to force Excel to create a square chart; or hold down Ctrl to make the chart align precisely with the underlying cell grid).

Release the mouse button to confirm the process. The first ChartWizard dialog appears. Do the following:

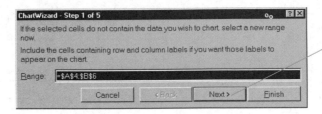

Click here

There are four more dialogs to complete. These ask you to specify the chart type and sub-format. You're also asked to confirm various layout issues. Complete each dialog as appropriate, then click Next. Finally, complete the last ChartWizard dialog and do the following:

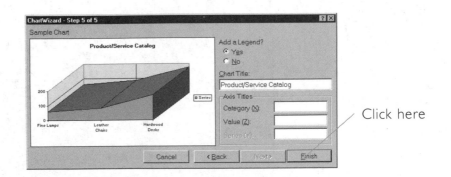

Click here

Excel now generates the chart.

Creating a separate chart sheet

First, select the cells you want converted into a chart. Pull down the Insert menu and click Chart, followed by As New Sheet. The first ChartWizard dialog appears. Do the following:

When you select the data cells, include a row or column of text entries if you want these inserted into the chart as descriptive labels.

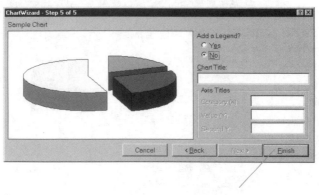

Click here

There are four more dialogs to complete. These ask you to specify the chart type and sub-format. You're also asked to confirm various layout issues. Complete each dialog as appropriate, then click Next. Finally, complete the last ChartWizard dialog and do the following:

Click here

Excel now generates the chart.

Working with pictures

HANDY TIP

Once inserted into a worksheet, pictures can be resized and moved in the normal way.

Most worksheets benefit from the inclusion of colour or greyscale pictures. These can be:

- output from other programs (e.g. drawings and illustrations)

- commercial clip art

- photographs

Excel will happily translate a wide variety of third-party graphics formats.

Inserting a picture

Position the insertion point at the location in the active worksheet where you want the picture to appear. Pull down the Insert menu and click Picture. Now carry out the following steps:

REMEMBER

Excel provides a preview of what the picture will look like when it's been imported. See the Preview box on the right of the dialog.

2 Click here. In the drop-down list, click the drive/folder which hosts the picture

4 Click here

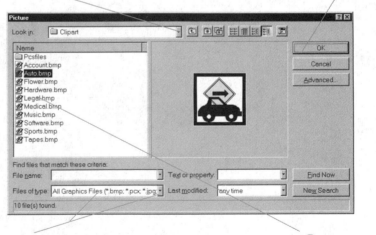

| Make sure All Graphics Files is shown. If it isn't, click the arrow and select it from the drop-down list

3 Click the picture file

Page setup - an overview

Making sure your worksheets print with the correct page setup can be a complex issue, for the simple reason that most worksheets become very extensive with the passage of time (so large, in fact, that in the normal course of things they won't fit onto a single page).

Page setup features you can customise include:

Charts in separate chart sheets have unique page setup options - see later.

- the paper size and orientation

- scaling

- the starting page number

- the print quality

- margins

- header/footer information

- page order

- which worksheet components print

Margin settings you can amend are:

- top

- bottom

- left

- right

Additionally, you can set the distance between the top page edge and the top of the header, and the distance between the bottom page edge and the bottom edge of the footer).

When you save your active workbook, all Page Setup settings are saved with it.

Setting page options

Excel comes with 11 pre-defined paper sizes which you can apply to your worksheets, in either portrait (top-to-bottom) or landscape (sideways on) orientation. This is one approach to effective printing. Another is scaling: you can print out your worksheets as they are, or you can have Excel shrink them so that they fit a given paper size (you can even automate this process). Additionally, you can set the print resolution and starting page number.

Using the Page tab in the Page Setup dialog

Pull down the File menu and click Page Setup. Now carry out step 1 below, followed by steps 2-6 as appropriate. Finally, carry out step 7:

HANDY TIP

Re step 5 - by default, Excel numbers pages from '1'. Leave the First Page Number field setting as Auto if you want this.

HANDY TIP

To make your worksheet print in a specific number of pages, complete the Fit to field.

1 Ensure the Page tab is active

2 Click the orientation you need

3 Click here; click the page size you need in the drop-down list

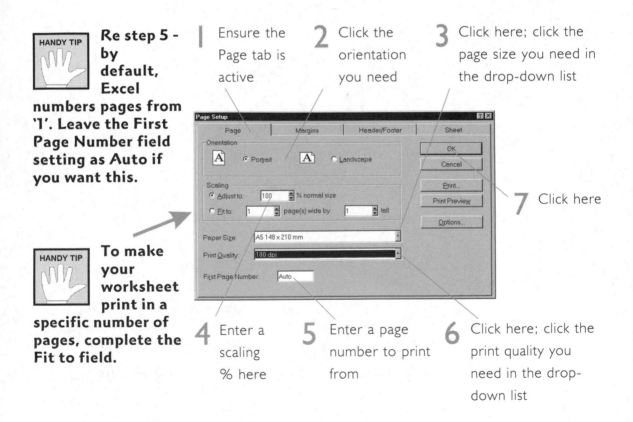

7 Click here

4 Enter a scaling % here

5 Enter a page number to print from

6 Click here; click the print quality you need in the drop-down list

Setting margin options

Excel lets you set a variety of margin settings. The illustration below shows the main ones:

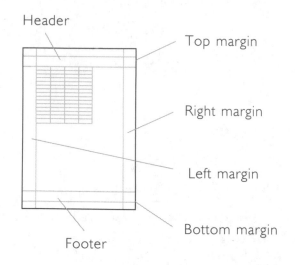

Header

Top margin

Right margin

Left margin

Bottom margin

Footer

Using the Margins tab in the Page Setup dialog

Pull down the File menu and click Page Setup. Now carry out step 1 below, followed by steps 2-3 as appropriate. Finally, carry out step 4:

1 Ensure the Margins tab is active

4 Click here

To specify how your worksheet aligns on the page, click either option here:

HANDY TIP

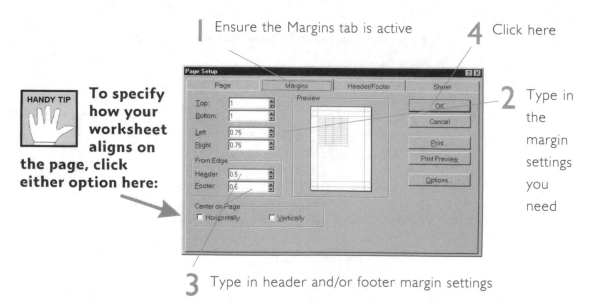

2 Type in the margin settings you need

3 Type in header and/or footer margin settings

Setting header/footer options

Excel provides a list of built-in header and footer settings. You can apply any of these to the active worksheet. These settings include:

- the worksheet title

- the workbook title

- the date

- the user's name

- 'confidential'

- permutations of these

Using the Header/Footer tab in the Page Setup dialog

Pull down the File menu and click Page Setup. Now carry out step 1 below, followed by steps 2-3 as appropriate. Finally, carry out step 4:

1 Ensure the Header/ Footer tab is active

2 Click here; select a header from the list

4 Click here

3 Click here; select a footer from the list

Page Setup

| Page | Margins | Header/Footer | Sheet |

Product and Service Catalog

OK

Cancel

Header:
Product and Service Catalog

Print...

Print Preview

Custom Header... Custom Footer...

Options...

Footer:
Page 1

Page 1

Setting sheet options

Excel lets you:

- define a printable area on-screen

- define a column or row title which will print on every page

- specify which worksheet components should print

- print with minimal formatting

- determine the print direction

Using the Sheet tab in the Page Setup dialog

Pull down the File menu and click Page Setup. Now carry out step 1 below, followed by steps 2-4 (and the tips) as appropriate. Finally, carry out step 5.

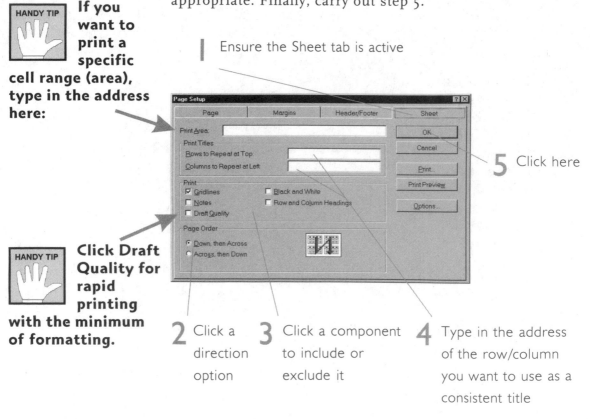

HANDY TIP

If you want to print a specific cell range (area), type in the address here:

1 Ensure the Sheet tab is active

5 Click here

HANDY TIP

Click Draft Quality for rapid printing with the minimum of formatting.

2 Click a direction option

3 Click a component to include or exclude it

4 Type in the address of the row/column you want to use as a consistent title

Page setup for charts

You can only print a chart separately if it's contained in a separate chart sheet (not if it's embedded within a worksheet).

Most page setup issues for charts in chart sheets are identical to those for worksheet data. The main difference, however, is that the Page Setup dialog has a Chart tab (rather than a Sheet tab).

In the Chart tab, you can opt to have the chart

• printed at full size

• scaled to fit the page

• user-defined

You can also set the print quality.

Using the Chart tab in the Page Setup dialog

Click the relevant chart tab in the worksheet tab area. Pull down the File menu and click Page Setup. Now carry out step 1 below, followed by steps 2-3 as appropriate. Finally, carry out step 4.

Re step 3 - clicking Custom ensures that, when you return to the chart sheet, the chart size can be adjusted with the mouse in the normal way. The chart then prints at whatever size you set.

Ensure the Chart tab is active

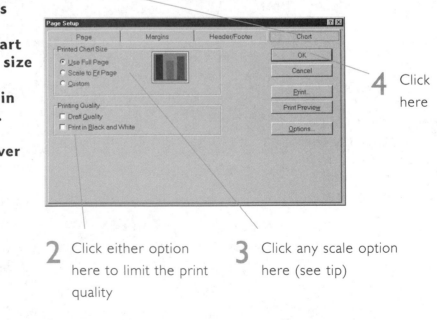

4 Click here

2 Click either option here to limit the print quality

3 Click any scale option here (see tip)

Launching Print Preview

Excel provides a special view mode called Print Preview. This displays the active worksheet exactly as it will look when printed. Use Print Preview as a final check just before you begin printing.

You can perform the following actions from within Print Preview:

- move from page to page

- zoom in or out on the active page

- adjust most Page Setup settings

- adjust margins visually

Launching Print Preview

Pull down the File menu and click Print Preview. This is the result:

HANDY TIP

To leave Print Preview mode and return to your worksheet (or chart sheet), simply press Esc.

Special Print Preview toolbar

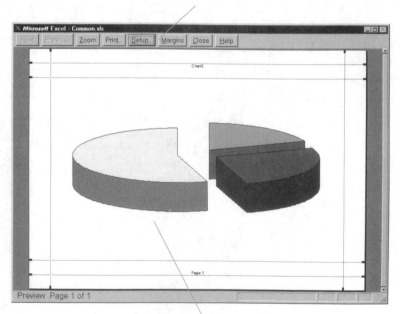

A preview of a chart sheet

Working with Print Preview

All of the operations you can perform in Print Preview mode can be accessed via the toolbar.

Using the Print Preview toolbar

Do any of the following, as appropriate:

REMEMBER

Excel's Print Preview mode has only two Zoom settings: Full Page and High-Magnification.

HANDY TIP

Re step 6 - see earlier topics (pages 117-122) for how to use the Page Setup dialog.

1 Click here to jump to the next page

3 Click here to zoom in or out

6 Click here to launch the Page Setup dialog

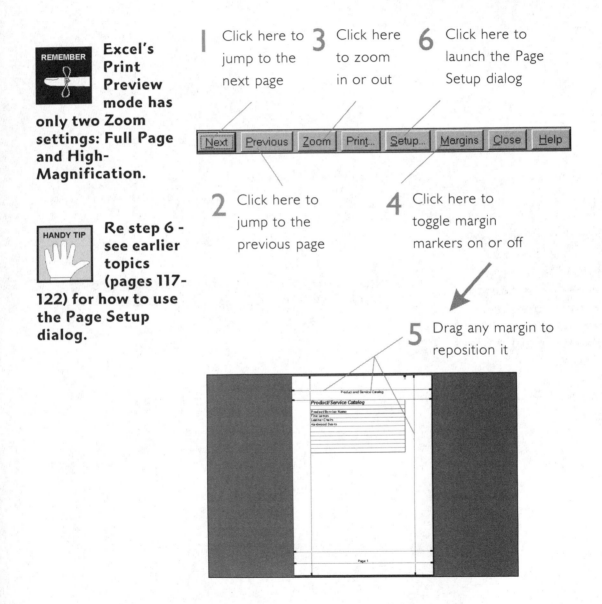

2 Click here to jump to the previous page

4 Click here to toggle margin markers on or off

5 Drag any margin to reposition it

Printing worksheet data

Excel lets you specify:

- the number of copies you want printed

- whether you want the copies 'collated'. This is the process whereby Excel prints one full copy at a time. For instance, if you're printing three copies of a 10-page worksheet, Excel prints pages 1-10 of the first copy, followed by pages 1-10 of the second and pages 1-10 of the third.

- which pages (or page ranges) you want printed

- whether you want the print run restricted to cells you selected before initiating printing

To select and print more than one worksheet, hold down Shift as you click on multiple tabs in the worksheet tab area.

You can 'mix and match' these, as appropriate.

Starting a print run

Open the workbook that contains the data you want to print. If you want to print an entire worksheet, click the relevant tab in the worksheet tab area. If you need to print a specific cell range within a worksheet, select it. Then pull down the File menu and click Print. Do any of steps 1-5. Then carry out step 6 to begin printing.

If you need to adjust your printer's internal settings before you initiate printing, click Properties. Then refer to your printer's manual.

1 Click here; select the printer you want from the list

2 Click the correct selection option

3 Type in the number of copies required

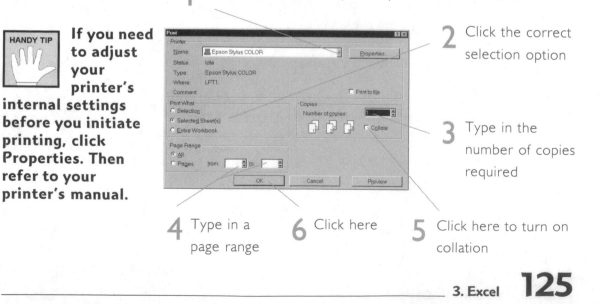

4 Type in a page range

6 Click here

5 Click here to turn on collation

Printing - the fast track approach

In earlier topics, we've looked at how to customise print options to meet varying needs and worksheet sizes. However, Excel – like Word – recognises that there will be times when you won't need this level of complexity. There are occasions when you'll merely want to print out your work – often for proofing purposes – with the standard print defaults applying.

These are:

- Excel prints only the active worksheet

- Excel prints only 1 copy

- Excel prints all pages within the active worksheet

- collation is turned off

For this reason, Excel provides a method which bypasses the standard Print dialog, and is therefore much quicker and easier to use.

Printing with the default print options

First, click the tab that relates to the worksheet you want to print. Ensure your printer is ready. Make sure the Standard toolbar is visible. (If it isn't, pull down the View menu and click Toolbars. In the Toolbars section of the Toolbars dialog, click Standard. Then click OK.) Now do the following:

Click here

Excel starts printing the active worksheet immediately.

PowerPoint

Use this chapter to acquire the basics of producing your own slide show. You'll learn how to use the AutoContent Wizard to automate the creation of a presentation, and how to customise it for your own use later. Finally, you'll print out (optional) and run your presentation.

Covers

The PowerPoint screen

Below is a detailed illustration of the PowerPoint screen.

Title bar   Menu bar   Rulers

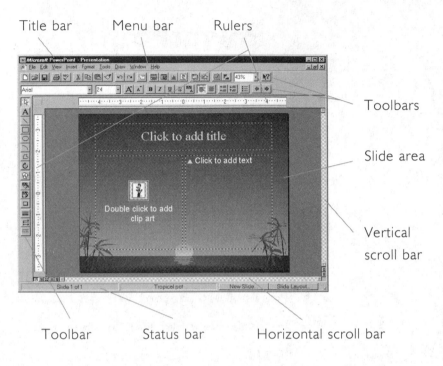

Toolbars

Slide area

Vertical scroll bar

Toolbar   Status bar   Horizontal scroll bar

Two of these components can be hidden, if required.

Specifying which screen components display

Pull down the Tools menu and click Options. Then:

Ensure the View tab is active

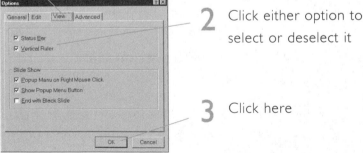

2 Click either option to select or deselect it

3 Click here

The AutoContent Wizard

In Section 1, we looked at how to create new Office documents based on templates and Wizards. PowerPoint has a unique and particularly detailed Wizard which handles the basics of creating a presentation.

Creating a new presentation with the AutoContent Wizard

Pull down the File menu and click New. Now do the following:

Ensure the Presentations tab is active

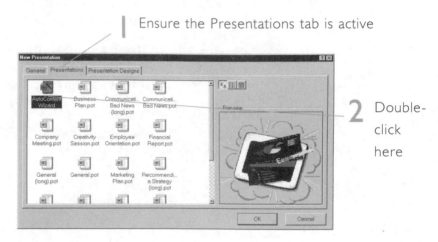

2 Double-click here

PowerPoint now launches the Wizard. Do the following:

The Wizard produces a 'standard' slide show which you can amend later, if you want.

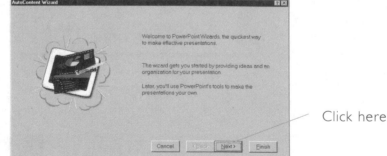

Click here

Complete the remaining dialogs in the normal way. In the final AutoContent dialog, click Finish to have PowerPoint generate the presentation.

The slide views - an overview

PowerPoint has the following views:

Slide	displays each slide individually
Outline	shows the underlying textual structure of the presentation
Slide Sorter	shows all the slides as icons, so you can manipulate them more easily
Notes Pages	shows each slide together with any speaker's notes

These are different ways of looking at your presentation. The best way to work with presentations is to use a combination of all four, as appropriate.

Switching to a view

Pull down the View menu and click Slide, Outline, Slide Sorter or Notes Pages.

The four views are shown below:

Slide View

Outline View

Slide Sorter View

Notes Pages View

Using the slide views

The following are some brief supplemental notes on how best to use the PowerPoint views.

Slide view

Slide view displays the current slide in its own window. Use Slide view when you want a detailed picture of a slide (for instance, when you amend any of the slide contents, or when you change the overall formatting).

To switch from slide to slide, you can press Page Up or Page Down as appropriate. For more information on how to move around in presentations, see 'Moving through presentations' later.

Outline view

HANDY TIP

All the views have their own default magnification. You can adjust this, however; simply pull down the View menu and click Zoom. In the Zoom dialog, type in a zoom % in the Percent field and click OK.

If you're currently only working with the text in a given presentation, use Outline view. Outline view provides an overview of slide structure and content. If a slide contains pictures, these display as filled icons (when a slide is empty of pictures, the icon is blank).

Slide Sorter view

If you need to rearrange the order of slides, use Slide Sorter view. You can simply click on a slide and drag it to a new location (to move more than one slide, hold down one Shift key as you click on them, then drag). You can also copy a slide by holding down Ctrl instead of Shift as you drag.

Notes Pages view

This view is an aid to the presenter rather than the viewer of the slide show. If you want to enter speaker's notes on a slide (for later printing), use Notes Pages view.

In Notes Pages view, the slide is displayed at a reduced size at the top of the page. Below this is a standard PowerPoint text object. For how to enter notes in this, see the 'Adding text to slides' topic later.

Customising slide structure

The easiest way to customise the basic format of a slide is to use AutoLayout. AutoLayout offers a selection of 24 layout structures and lets you apply your choice to a specific slide or group of slides. When you've done this, you can then amend the individual components (see later topics).

Using AutoLayout

Make sure you're in Slide or Slide Sorter view. If you're in Slide Sorter view, click the slide(s) you want to amend. Pull down the Format menu and click Slide Layout. Then do the following:

HANDY TIP

You can select more than one slide in Slide Sorter view by holding down one Shift key as you click on the slide icons.

Click a slide format

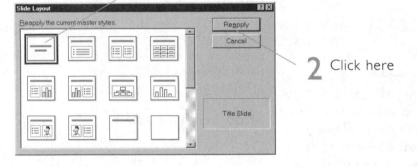

2 Click here

Any slide components present before you applied the new format will still remain. However, they may need to be resized or moved. Look at the illustration below:

HANDY TIP

Standard mouse techniques can be used to reposition or rescale text objects in PowerPoint.

The imposition of the new format has meant that this text is now in the wrong location

Adding text to slides

When you create a new slide show (unless you choose to create a blank presentation), PowerPoint fills each slide with placeholders containing sample text. The idea is that you should replace this with your own text.

The illustration below shows a sample slide before customisation:

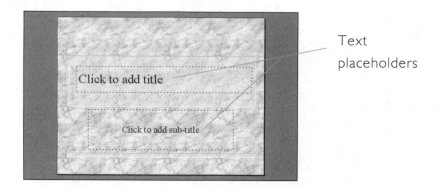

Text placeholders

To insert your own text, click in any text placeholder. PowerPoint displays a text entry box. Now do the following:

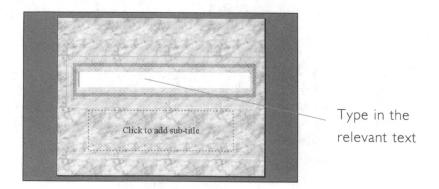

Type in the relevant text

Finally, click anywhere outside the placeholder to confirm the addition of the new text.

Formatting text (1)

You can carry out a variety of formatting enhancements on text. You can:

- change the font and/or typesize

- apply a font style or effect

- apply a colour

- specify the alignment

- specify the line spacing

Font-based formatting

Click inside the relevant text object and select the text you want to format. Pull down the Format menu and click Font. Now carry out any of steps 1-6 below, as appropriate. Then follow step 7:

1 Click a new typeface

2 Type in a new point size

7 Click here

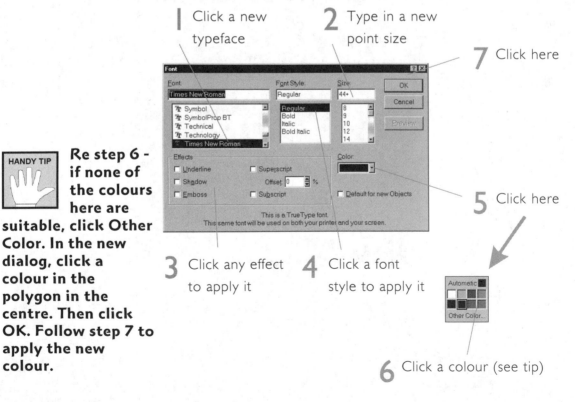

5 Click here

3 Click any effect to apply it

4 Click a font style to apply it

6 Click a colour (see tip)

HANDY TIP **Re step 6 – if none of the colours here are suitable, click Other Color. In the new dialog, click a colour in the polygon in the centre. Then click OK. Follow step 7 to apply the new colour.**

Formatting text (2)

Changing text spacing

First, click inside the relevant text object and select the text whose spacing you want to amend. Pull down the Format menu and click Line Spacing. Now carry out any of steps 1-3 below, as appropriate. Then follow step 4.

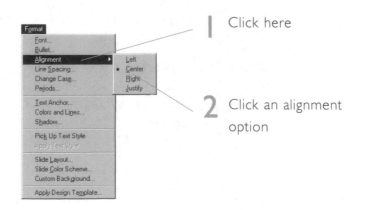

Type in a line spacing

4 Click here

2 Enter an after-paragraph spacing

3 Enter a pre-paragraph spacing

Changing text alignment

First, click inside the relevant text object and select the text whose alignment you want to amend. Pull down the Format menu and do the following:

Click here

2 Click an alignment option

Moving through presentations

Since presentations – by their very nature – always have more than one slide, it's essential to be able to move from slide to slide easily (it's even more essential in the case of especially large presentations). There are two main methods you can use to do this.

Using the vertical scroll bar

In Slide or Notes Pages views, move the mouse pointer over the vertical scroll box. Hold down the left mouse button and drag the box up or down. As you do so, PowerPoint displays a message box giving you the number and title of the slide you're up to.

 Of course, you can also click the vertical scroll bar arrows to move through your presentation in the normal way. However, the page number message doesn't then display.

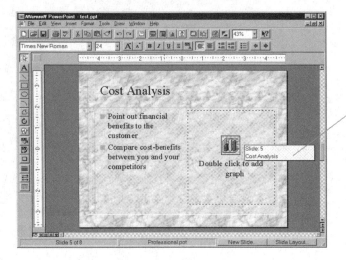

Slide number indicator

When the correct number displays, release the mouse button to jump to that slide.

Using Slide Sorter view

Slide Sorter view offers a useful shortcut which you can use to jump immediately to a specific slide. Simply double-click any slide icon within Slide Sorter view; PowerPoint then switches to Slide view with the slide you selected displayed.

Inserting & deleting slides

You'll often want to insert a slide within the body of a presentation. There are also occasions when you'll need to delete a slide because it's no longer required. PowerPoint lets you do both easily and conveniently.

Inserting a slide

In Slide view or Notes Pages view, move to the slide that you want to precede the new one. In Outline view, triple-click the slide that you want to precede the new one. In Slide Sorter view, click the relevant slide. Then pull down the Insert menu and click New Slide.

Now do the following:

The current slide format is highlighted; click another if you want to apply a new format

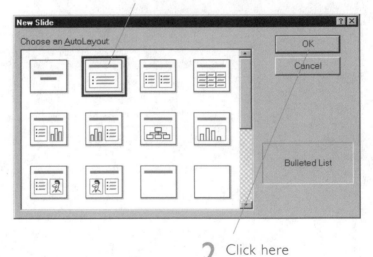

2 Click here

When you delete a slide, PowerPoint does not provide a message requiring your confirmation. The slide and its contents are erased immediately.

Deleting a slide

In Slide view or Notes Pages view, move to the slide that you want to delete. In Outline view, triple-click the slide. In Slide Sorter view, click it (or hold down one Shift key as you click on multiple slide icons to delete more than one slide). Then pull down the Edit menu and click Delete Slide.

Inserting pictures (1)

Pictures can help enormously in making your presentations visually effective. You can add pictures in two basic ways.

Adding clip art

If the Office Clip Art Gallery is installed on your computer, you can do the following. Go to the slide into which you want the clip art added. Pull down the Insert menu and click Clip Art. Now carry out the following steps:

Click a category

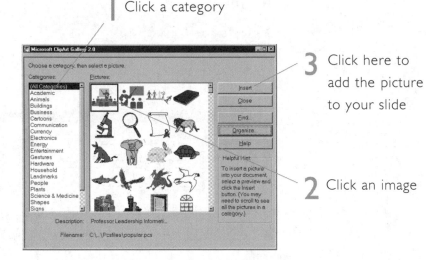

3 Click here to add the picture to your slide

2 Click an image

A slide with an added clip-art image:

Inserting pictures (2)

Third party images can be very useful in slides. They can be:

- output from other programs (e.g. drawings and illustrations)

- commercial clip art

- photographs

PowerPoint will happily translate a wide variety of third-party graphics formats.

HANDY TIP **Once inserted into a slide,** pictures can be resized and moved in the normal way.

Adding a third-party picture

To insert a picture produced by another program, do the following. Go to the slide into which you want the clip art added. Pull down the Insert menu and click Picture. Now carry out the following steps:

2 Click here. In the drop-down list, click the drive/folder that hosts the picture

4 Click here

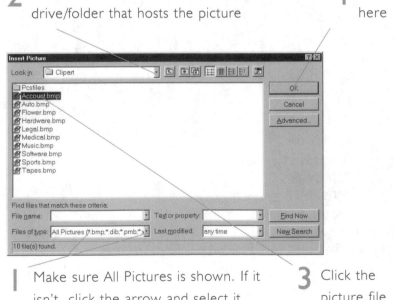

1 Make sure All Pictures is shown. If it isn't, click the arrow and select it from the drop-down list

3 Click the picture file

Printing

You can print any presentation component. These include:

- slides

- notes

- outlines

PowerPoint makes printing easy.

Printing a presentation

Pull down the File menu and click Print. Now carry out any of steps 1-5 below, as appropriate. Finally, follow step 6.

Click here; select the printer you want from the list

2 Click here to print the current slide only

3 Type in the number of copies required

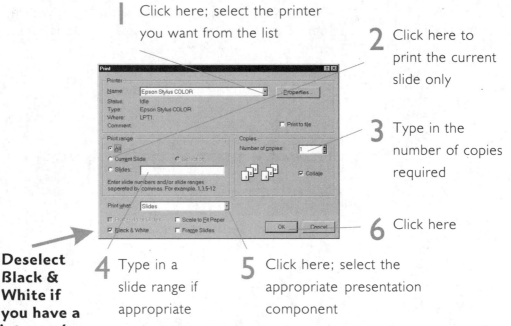

6 Click here

Deselect Black & White if you have a colour printer and want to print out in colour.

4 Type in a slide range if appropriate

5 Click here; select the appropriate presentation component

Fast-track printing

To print using all the default settings, without launching the Print dialog, simply click the Print button on the Standard toolbar:

Running a presentation (1)

Once you've created (and possibly printed) your slide show, it's time to run it. Before you do so, however, you should set the run parameters.

When you run your presentation you can, if you want, have PowerPoint wait for your command before moving from slide to slide. This is useful if you anticipate being interrupted during the presentation. You retain full control over delivery.

Alternatively, you can have the slide show run automatically. Before you can do this, though, you have to 'rehearse' the intervals between slides you want. The rehearsal process is a dummy run during which you tell PowerPoint how long each interval between slides should be.

Preparing to run your slide show

First, open the presentation you want to run. Then pull down the View menu and click Slide Show. Now do the following:

1 If you don't want all slides to run, enter start and end slide numbers

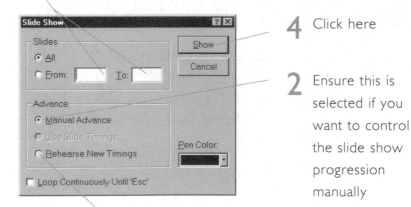

4 Click here

2 Ensure this is selected if you want to control the slide show progression manually

3 Click here if you want the slide show progression to be automatic

Running a presentation (2)

If you want to jump directly to a specific slide, type the number and press Return.

Running the presentation manually

If you followed steps 2 and 4 on page 141 (and optionally step 1), PowerPoint runs the first slide of your presentation straight away. When you're ready to move on to the next slide, left-click once (or press Page Down). If you need to go back to the previous slide, right-click once; in the menu that appears, click Previous. Or simply press Page Up.

Running the presentation automatically

If you followed steps 3 and 4 on page 141 (and optionally step 1), PowerPoint launches the first slide, together with a special timer box. Do the following:

If you want to end your slide show at any time, simply press Esc. This applies to manual and automatic presentations.

This timer counts the interval until the next slide; when the timing is right, follow step 2

2 Click here

After step 2, PowerPoint moves to the next slide. Repeat steps 1 and 2 until all the slides have had intervals allocated. Finally, another message appears:

Click here to confirm the timings you've allocated

PowerPoint returns to your open presentation. To run your slide show automatically, pull down the View menu and click Slide Show. In the Slide Show dialog, click Use Slide Timings, followed by Show. PowerPoint now runs the slide show, progressing from slide to slide under its own steam.

Schedule+

This chapter provides a brief introduction to the *stand-alone* (i.e. non-workgroup) use of Schedule+. Use it to learn how to work with the interrelated schedule tabs. You'll enter appointments/events, tasks and contact details; Schedule+ will then coordinate them so that you can manage your business/personal affairs more easily.

Covers

The Schedule+ screen

Below is a detailed illustration of the Schedule+ screen.

Title bar   Menu bar   Toolbar

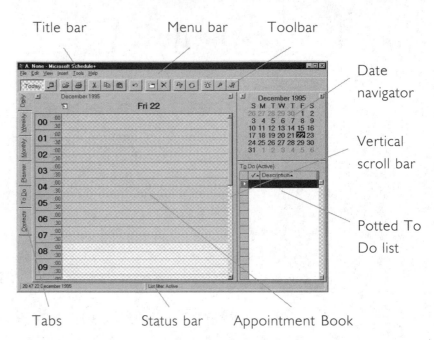

Date navigator

Vertical scroll bar

Potted To Do list

Tabs   Status bar   Appointment Book

Some of these – e.g. the menu and scroll bars – are standard to just about all programs that run under Windows. However, you can make more tabs visible, if you wish.

Specifying which tabs display

Pull down the View menu and click Tab Gallery. Then:

Repeat steps 1 and 2 for as many tabs as you want to make visible. Then follow step 3.

To hide a tab, click it in the Show these tabs field. Click Remove. Then follow step 3.

Click the tab you want to add

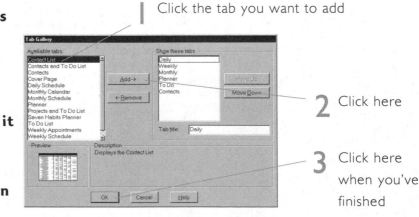

2 Click here

3 Click here when you've finished

Logging on

When you run Schedule+, the first stage is to 'log on'. This process allows you to access your personal schedule. Do the following.

Schedule+ Logon

Type the appropriate logon name for the schedule you want to work with.

User name: A. None

OK   Cancel   Help

1 Type your name here

2 Click here

If you've used it before, Schedule+ now launches. However, if this is the first time you've run Schedule+, a special message appears. Carry out the following steps:

Microsoft Schedule+

Welcome to Schedule+ 7.0

Schedule+ could not locate your schedule file. Before you use Schedule+, you should choose a schedule file.

● **I want to create a new schedule file**
If you have never used Schedule+ before, create a new schedule file.

○ **I want to use an existing schedule file**
If you have managed your time with Schedule+ before, pick your schedule file.

OK   Cancel

1 Ensure this is selected

2 Click here

Now do the following to create a new schedule file:

Select Local Schedule

Save in: Schedule

Routine.SCD

File name: New   Save

Save as type: Schedule+ 7.0 (*.SCD)   Cancel

Help

1 Type in a filename

2 Click here

REMEMBER

Schedule files have the extension SCD.

Schedule tabs - an overview

The Schedule+ tabs provide alternative ways of viewing and interacting with your schedules. The following tabs appear by default in the Schedule+ window:

Daily Switches to Daily view. An aspect of the Appointment Book; used to enter appointments and events on a daily basis.

Weekly Switches to Weekly view. An aspect of the Appointment Book; used to enter appointments and events on a weekly basis.

Monthly Switches to Monthly view. An aspect of the Appointment Book, useful for obtaining an overview and for inserting appointments.

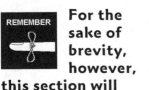

See the 'Working with the To Do list' topic later for how to prioritise tasks.

Planner Switches to the Planner. A directory of personal meetings.

To Do Switches to the To Do list. A directory of prioritised tasks/assignments

Contacts Switches to Contacts view. A list of names, telephone numbers and other important business/personal data.

Some aspects of Schedule+ – for instance, the use of the Planner to coordinate meetings among workgroup members – are beyond the scope of this book.

For the sake of brevity, however, this section will only discuss each operation once, in situ.

Much of the usefulness of Schedule+ as an organising aid lies in the way in which the various views are intimately connected. For example, if you set yourself a task in the To Do list, it becomes visible in the abbreviated To Do list in the Daily tab. In the same way, any event you schedule in the Daily tab also appears in the Weekly and Monthly tabs, as appropriate . . .

It's possible to perform just about any scheduling action from within any view.

Working with the Daily view (1)

You can add appointments to the Daily tab.

Use the Daily tab as the most convenient way to enter appointments.

You can stipulate the following:

- that the appointment is 'recurring' (this means that it's automatically entered in your Appointment Book each year)

- that the appointment is 'tentative' (in other words, it's greyed out in the Appointment book)

Adding an appointment

Carry out steps 1, 2 and 3 below (and optionally, steps 4 and 5):

Re step 2 – if the date shown in the Date Navigator isn't correct, click the following: ◀ **or** ▶ **to go back or forward by one month respectively.**

Re step 3 – if you need to amend or update an existing appointment, type in revised details.

4 Click here to make the appointment recurring

5 Click here to make the appointment private

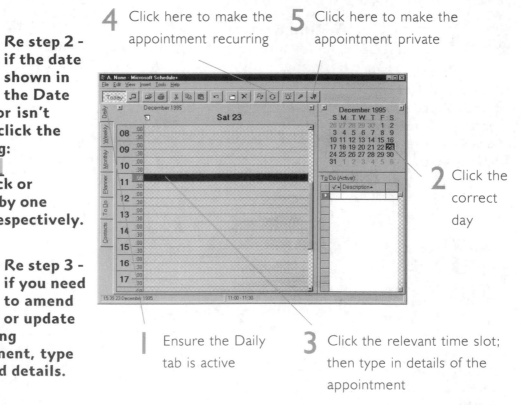

2 Click the correct day

1 Ensure the Daily tab is active

3 Click the relevant time slot; then type in details of the appointment

Working with the Daily view (2)

You can add events to the Daily tab.

Schedule+ handles events in a rather different way to appointments. For example, they don't occupy specific time slots in your Appointment Book. Instead, they can relate to any day and can even extend over more than one.

Schedule+ distinguishes between events and annual events. Annual events occur yearly on a specific date.

Examples of events include:

*   birthdays and anniversaries

*   shows

*   seminars

If you need to amend or update an existing event, double-click its entry at the top of the Appointment Book. Then follow steps 1-3 here, as appropriate.

Events appear at the top of the Appointment Book.

Adding an event

Pull down the Insert menu and click Event. Now do the following:

Type in start and end dates

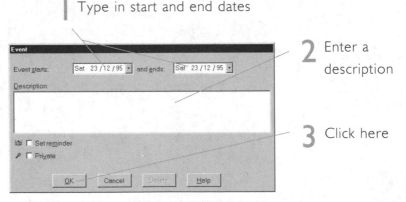

2 Enter a description

3 Click here

Re step 1 - for an annual event, instead of a start and end date, simply type in the date on which you want the annual event to recur.

Adding an annual event

Pull down the Insert menu and click Annual Event. The dialog that appears is almost identical to the above illustration. Simply follow the steps in 'Adding an event' earlier (but see the tip).

Working with the Weekly view

The Weekly view is an alternative way to display your appointments and events.

By default, Schedule+ displays 5 days in Weekly view. If you want, you can easily change this. If, however, you display one day, Schedule+ changes to Daily view (minus the Date Navigator and To Do list).

In Weekly view, you can enter appointments and events in the same way that you can in Daily view – see 'Working with the Daily view (1)' and 'Working with the Daily view (2)' for how to do this.

Changing the number of days displayed

Pull down the View menu and click Number of Days. In the sub-menu which launches, click 1, 2, 3, 4, 5, 6 or 7.

Moving around in Weekly view

You can jump to a specific date in Weekly view. To do this, make sure the Toolbar is displayed. (If it isn't, pull down the View menu and click Toolbar.) Do the following:

Click here

This is the result. Carry out the following steps:

1 (Optional) Click here to move 1 month back

2 (Optional) Click here to move 1 month forward

3 Click the day you want to view

Working with the Monthly view

To move to a new date in Monthly view, follow the method outlined in 'Moving around in Weekly view' in the 'Working with the Weekly view' topic.

Use Monthly view to gain a useful overview of your schedule.

You can't, however, use it to insert appointments directly because the scale is too small. Instead, use the following method.

Inserting a new appointment

Pull down the Insert menu and click Appointment. Then carry out steps 1-4 and 7 below (steps 5 and 6 are optional):

1 Ensure the General tab is active

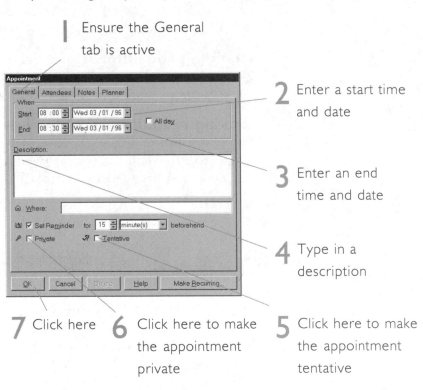

2 Enter a start time and date

3 Enter an end time and date

4 Type in a description

7 Click here

6 Click here to make the appointment private

5 Click here to make the appointment tentative

Inserting an event

You can insert events in Monthly view by using the same techniques as for Daily view. See 'Adding an event' and 'Adding an annual event' in the 'Working with the Daily view' topic.

Working with the Planner

Use the Planner to obtain a useful overview of your appointments. Look at the illustration below:

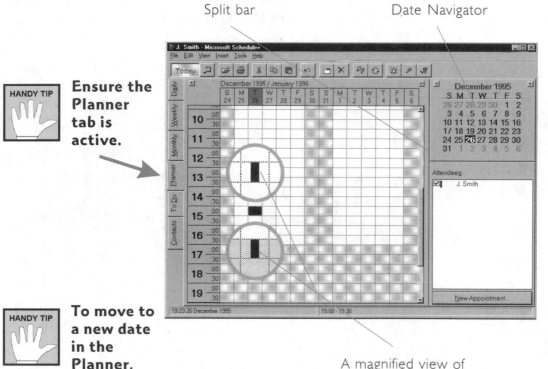

Split bar   Date Navigator

HANDY TIP

Ensure the Planner tab is active.

A magnified view of two appointments

HANDY TIP

To move to a new date in the Planner, use the Date Navigator.

The vertical blocks denote appointments entered into Schedule+.

Resizing the Planner window

You can increase or decrease the size of the Planner window by dragging the split bar (see the illustration). To do this, position the mouse pointer over the split bar. Click and hold down the left mouse button; drag the bar to the left, to display fewer days, or to the right to display more. Release the button to confirm the operation.

Working with the To Do list

Use the To Do list to enter and track tasks.

Tasks in the To Do list are associated with specific dates. When you've entered a task into the To Do list, it displays in the abbreviated To Do list in Daily view.

Entering a task

If the To Do list isn't already active, click the To Do tab in the Schedule+ window. Then do the following:

If you need to amend or update an existing task, click its row. Then follow steps 1-3.

Click the row into which you want to insert the new task

Task headings

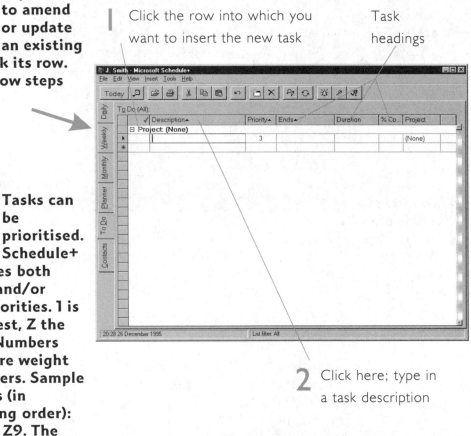

Tasks can be prioritised. Schedule+ recognises both number and/or letter priorities. 1 is the highest, Z the lowest. Numbers carry more weight than letters. Sample priorities (in descending order): 9, A, B7, Z9. The default priority is 3.

2 Click here; type in a task description

Now complete the remaining fields (as appropriate) by clicking on the task headings and making the appropriate choice(s) from the drop-down lists.

Working with the Contacts view

Use the Contacts view as a convenient place to keep track of business/personal contacts.

Schedule+ displays contacts in two forms:

- as a grid

- using a business card model

You can enter contacts directly into either, but it's easier to do so into the business card section.

Entering a contact

If the Contacts view isn't already active, click the Contacts tab in the Schedule+ window. Then do the following:

HANDY TIP

If you need to amend a contact, click it in the Contact grid. Then carry out steps 2-4 as appropriate.

HANDY TIP

Repeat steps 1-4 for each contact whose details you want to insert.

1 Click a button here to start a new row

2 Click the appropriate tab

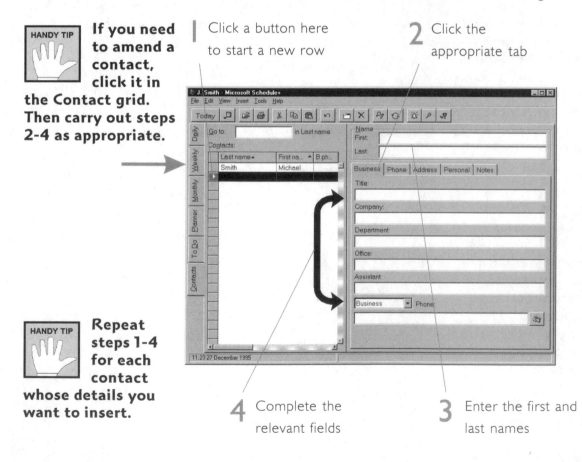

4 Complete the relevant fields

3 Enter the first and last names

Printing

If you need to print out your schedule, you can specify the following:

- the print layout (i.e. which tab components print, and in which form)

- the print quality and font size

- the paper format

- the appropriate date range

- the margins (the default is 1")

Printing your schedule

Pull down the File menu and click Print. Now carry out steps 1-6 below as appropriate. Finally, follow step 7.

 To see what your schedule looks like before you initiate printing, click Preview. To return to the Print dialog, press Esc.

 To set revised margins and/or your printer's internal settings, click Setup. Then complete the Print Setup dialog accordingly. Click OK. Now follow step 7 here to print your schedule.

1 Click a print layout

2 Click here; click a print quality in the list

3 Click here; click a font size in the list

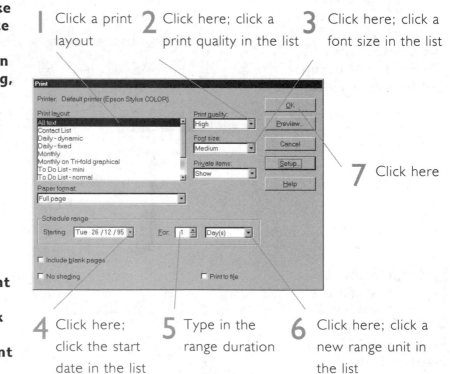

7 Click here

4 Click here; click the start date in the list

5 Type in the range duration

6 Click here; click a new range unit in the list

Index